THE ANTICHRIST

Titles on Ethics in Prometheus's Philosophy of Religion Series

See the back of this volume for a complete list of titles in Prometheus's Great Books in Philosophy and Great Minds series.

THE ANTICHRIST

FRIEDRICH NIETZSCHE

Translated by Anthony M. Ludovici

GREAT BOOKS IN PHILOSOPHY

PB Prometheus Books
59 John Glenn Drive
Amherst, New York 14228-2197

Published 2000 by Prometheus Books

Inquiries should be addressed to
Prometheus Books
59 John Glenn Drive
Amherst, New York 14228–2197

VOICE: 716–691–0133, EXT. 207; FAX: 716–564–2711.
WWW.PROMETHEUSBOOKS.COM

Library of Congress Cataloging-in-Publication Data

Nietzsche, Friedrich Wilehlm, 1844–1900.
    [Antichrist. English]
    The antichrist / Friedrich Nietzsche ; translated by Anthony M.
Ludovici.
        p. cm. — (Great books in philosophy)
    Originally published: Twilight of the idols, and, The Antichrist.
London ; New York : Macmillan, 1911.
    Includes bibliographical references.
    ISBN-13: 978–1–57392–832–8 (alk. paper)
    ISBN-10: 1–57392–832–1 (alk. paper)
    1. Christianity—Controversial literature. I. Ludovici, Antony Mario,
1882–1971. II. Title. III. Series.

B3313.A8ES 2000
193—dc21

                             00–056522
                             CIP

Printed in the United States of America on acid-free paper.

FRIEDRICH NIETZSCHE was born on October 15, 1844, to the family of a Protestant minister in the town of Rocken, which is located in the Saxony-Anhalt region of what is now eastern Germany. After studying philosophy in Bonn and Leipzig, Nietzsche became a professor at the University of Basel, Switzerland, in 1869. Later, he opted to become a Swiss citizen.

While working in Switzerland, he published his first book, a literary work titled *The Birth of Tragedy from the Spirit of Music*. This volume was produced during Nietzsche's friendship with the composer Richard Wagner, though only a few years would pass before the two would part ways as a result of personal and intellectual differences.

In failing health and unable to devote himself full time to both teaching and independent writing, Nietzsche chose to resign his university position. During the next decade he wrote such works as *Thus Spoke Zarathustra* (most of which appeared in 1883), *Beyond Good and Evil* (1886), *Geneology of Morals* (1887), *Twilight of the Gods* (1888), *Antichrist* (1888), and *Ecce Homo* (1888).

His collapse while in Turin, Italy, in early 1889, would prove the beginning of a long and arduous struggle with ill-health and insanity. Nietzsche died in the care of his family in Weimar on August 25, 1900, just a few weeks prior to his fifty-sixth birthday.

Nietzsche advocated the view that humankind should reject otherworldliness and instead rely on its own creative potential to discover values that best serve the social good. His infamous "superman" or "overman" is one who has recognized how to channel individual passions in the direction of creative outlets. In rejecting the morality of the masses, Nietzsche celebrates the pursuit of classical virtues.

PREFACE

THIS book belongs to the very few. Maybe not one of them is yet alive; unless he be of those who understand my Zarathustra. How *can* I confound myself with those who to-day already find a hearing?—Only the day after to-morrow belongs to me. Some are born posthumously.

I am only too well aware of the conditions under which a man understands me, and then *necessarily* understands. He must be intellectually upright to the point of hardness, in order even to endure my seriousness and my passion. He must be used to living on mountain-tops, — and to feeling the wretched gabble of politics and national egotism *beneath* him. He must have become indifferent; he must never inquire whether truth is profitable or whether it may prove fatal. . . . Possessing from strength a predilection for questions for which no one has enough courage nowadays; the courage for the *forbidden*; his predestination must be the labyrinth. The experience of seven solitudes. New ears for new music. New eyes for the most remote things. A new conscience for truths which hitherto have remained dumb. And the will to economy on a large scale: to husband his strength and his enthusiasm. . . . He must honour himself, he must love himself; he must be absolutely free with regard to himself. . . . Very well then! Such men alone are my readers, my proper readers, my preordained readers: of what account are the rest?—the rest are simply—humanity.—One must be superior to humanity in power, in loftiness of soul,—in contempt.

FRIEDRICH NIETZSCHE.

I

LET us look each other in the face. We are hyperboreans,—we know well enough how far outside
the crowd we stand. "Thou wilt find the way to the
Hyperboreans neither by land nor by water": Pindar
already knew this much about us. Beyond the north,
the ice, and death—*our life, our happiness.* . . . We
discovered happiness; we know the way; we found
the way out of thousands of years of labyrinth. Who
else would have found it?—Not the modern man,
surely?—"I do not know where I am or what I am
to do; I am everything that knows not where it is
or what to do,"—sighs the modern man. We were
made quite ill by *this* modernity,—with its indolent
peace, its cowardly compromise, and the whole of
the virtuous filth of its Yea and Nay. This toler-
ance and *largeur de cœur* which "forgives" everything because it "understands" everything, is a
Sirocco for us. We prefer to live amid ice than to
be breathed upon by modern virtues and other
southerly winds! . . . We were brave enough; we
spared neither ourselves nor others: but we were
very far from knowing whither to direct our bravery.
We were becoming gloomy; people called us fatal-
ists. *Our* fate—it was the abundance, the tension

and the storing up of power. We thirsted for
thunderbolts and great deeds ; we kept at the most
respectful distance from the joy of the weakling,
from "resignation." . . . Thunder was in our air,
that part of nature which we are, became overcast—
for we had no direction. The formula of our happiness : a Yea, a Nay, a straight line, a goal.

2

What is good ?   All that enhances the feeling of
power, the Will to Power, and power itself in man.
What is bad ?—All that proceeds from weakness.
What is happiness?—The feeling that power is
increasing,—that resistance has been overcome.

Not contentment, but more power; not peace at
any price, but war; not virtue, but efficiency* (virtue
in the Renaissance sense, *virtù*, free from all moralic
acid).   The weak and the botched shall perish : first
principle of our humanity.   And they ought even to
be helped to perish.

What is more harmful than any vice ?—Practical sympathy with all the botched and the weak—
Christianity.

3

The problem I set in this work is not what will
replace mankind in the order of living beings
(—Man is an *end--*); but, what type of man must
be *reared*, must be *willed*, as having the highest
value, as being the most worthy of life and the
surest guarantee of the future.

---

* The German "*Tüchtigkeit*" has a nobler ring than our
word "efficiency."—TR.

This more valuable type has appeared often enough already : but as a happy accident, as an exception, never as *willed*. He has rather been precisely the most feared ; hitherto he has been almost the terrible in itself ;—and from out the very fear he provoked there arose the will to rear the type which has now been reared, *attained :* the domestic animal, the gregarious animal, the sick animal man,—the Christian.

4

Mankind does *not* represent a development towards a better, stronger or higher type, in the sense in which this is supposed to occur to-day. " Progress " is merely a modern idea — that is to say, a false idea.* The modern European is still far below the European of the Renaissance in value. The process of evolution does not by any means imply elevation, enhancement and increasing strength.

On the other hand isolated and individual cases are continually succeeding in different places on earth, as the outcome of the most different cultures, and in these a *higher type* certainly manifests itself : something which by the side of mankind in general, represents a kind of superman. Such lucky strokes of great success have always been possible and will perhaps always be possible. And even whole races, tribes and nations may in certain circumstances represent such *lucky strokes.*

* *Cf.* Disraeli : " But enlightened Europe is not happy. Its existence is a fever which it calls progress. Progress to what ? " (" Tancred," Book III., Chap. vii.).—TR.

5

We must not deck out and adorn Christianity : it has waged a deadly war upon this *higher* type of man, it has set a ban upon all the fundamental instincts of this type, and has distilled evil and the devil himself out of these instincts:—the strong man as the typical pariah, the villain. Christianity has sided with everything weak, low, and botched ; it has made an ideal out of *antagonism* towards all the self-preservative instincts of strong life : it has corrupted even the reason of the strongest intellects, by teaching that the highest values of intellectuality are sinful, misleading and full of temptations. The most lamentable example of this was the corruption of Pascal, who believed in the perversion of his reason through original sin, whereas it had only been perverted by his Christianity.

6

A painful and ghastly spectacle has just risen before my eyes. I tore down the curtain which concealed mankind's *corruption*. This word in my mouth is at least secure from the suspicion that it contains a moral charge against mankind. It is—I would fain emphasise this again—free from moralic acid : to such an extent is this so, that I am most thoroughly conscious of the corruption in question precisely in those quarters in which hitherto people have aspired with most determination to " virtue " and to " godliness." As you have already surmised, I understand corruption in the sense of *decadence*. What I maintain is this, that all the values upon which mankind builds its highest hopes and desires are *decadent* values.

I call an animal, a species, an individual corrupt, when it loses its instincts, when it selects and *prefers* that which is detrimental to it. A history of the "higher feelings," of "human ideals"—and it is not impossible that I shall have to write it— would almost explain why man is so corrupt. Life itself, to my mind, is nothing more nor less than the instinct of growth, of permanence, of accumulating forces, of power: where the will to power is lacking, degeneration sets in. My contention is that all the highest values of mankind *lack* this will, —that the values of decline and of *nihilism* are exercising the sovereign power under the cover of the holiest names.

7

Christianity is called the religion of *pity*.—Pity is opposed to the tonic passions which enhance the energy of the feeling of life : its action is depressing. A man loses power when he pities. By means of pity the drain on strength which suffering itself already introduces into the world is multiplied a thousandfold. Through pity, suffering itself becomes infectious; in certain circumstances it may lead to a total loss of life and vital energy, which is absurdly out of proportion to the magnitude of the cause (—the case of the death of the Nazarene). This is the first standpoint; but there is a still more important one. Supposing one measures pity according to the value of the reactions it usually stimulates, its danger to life appears in a much more telling light. On the whole, pity thwarts the law

of development which is the law of selection. It
preserves that which is ripe for death, it fights in
favour of the disinherited and the condemned of
life; thanks to the multitude of abortions of all
kinds which it maintains in life, it lends life itself a
sombre and questionable aspect. People have dared
to call pity a virtue (—in every *noble* culture it is considered as a weakness—); people went still further,
they exalted it to *the* virtue, the root and origin of
all virtues,—but, of course, what must never be for-
gotten is the fact that this was done from the standpoint of a philosophy which was nihilistic, and on
whose shield the device *The Denial of Life* was
inscribed. Schopenhauer was right in this respect:
by means of pity, life is denied and made *more
worthy of denial*,—pity is the *praxis* of Nihilism. I
repeat, this depressing and infectious instinct thwarts
those instincts which aim at the preservation and
enhancement of the value life: by *multiplying* misery
quite as much as by preserving all that is miserable,
it is the principal agent in promoting decadence,—
pity exhorts people to nothing, to *nonentity!* But
they do not say "*nonentity*," they say "Beyond," or
"God," or "the true life"; or Nirvana, or Salvation,
or Blessedness, instead. This innocent rhetoric,
which belongs to the realm of the religio-moral
idiosyncrasy, immediately appears to be *very much
less innocent* if one realises what the tendency is
which here tries to drape itself in the mantle of
sublime expressions—the tendency of hostility to
life. Schopenhauer was hostile to life: that is why
he elevated pity to a virtue. . . . Aristotle, as
you know, recognised in pity a morbid and danger-

ous state, of which it was wise to rid one's self from time to time by a purgative: he regarded tragedy as a purgative. For the sake of the instinct of life, it would certainly seem necessary to find some means of lancing any such morbid and dangerous accumulation of pity, as that which possessed Schopenhauer (and unfortunately the whole of our literary and artistic decadence as well, from St Petersburg to Paris, from Tolstoi to Wagner), if only to make it *burst*. . . . Nothing is more unhealthy in the midst of our unhealthy modernity, than Christian pity. To be doctors *here*, to be inexorable *here*, to wield the knife effectively *here*,— all this is our business, all this is *our* kind of love to our fellows, this is what makes *us* philosophers, us hyperboreans !— —

8

It is necessary to state whom we regard as our antithesis :—the theologians, and all those who have the blood of theologians in their veins—the whole of our philosophy. . . . A man must have had his very nose upon this fatality, or better still he must have experienced it in his own soul ; he must almost have perished through it, in order to be unable to treat this matter lightly (—the free-spiritedness of our friends the naturalists and physiologists is, in my opinion, a *joke*,—what they lack in these questions is passion, what they lack is having suffered from these questions—). This poisoning extends much further than people think : I unearthed the " arrogant " instinct of the theologian, wherever nowadays people feel themselves idealists,

—wherever, thanks to superior antecedents, they claim the right to rise above reality and to regard it with suspicion. . . . Like the priest the idealist has every grandiloquent concept in his hand (—and not only in his hand!), he wields them all with kindly contempt against the "understanding," the "senses," "honours," "decent living," "science"; he regards such things as *beneath* him, as detrimental and seductive forces, upon the face of which, "the Spirit" moves in pure absoluteness :—as if humility, chastity, poverty, in a word *holiness*, had not done incalculably more harm to life hitherto, than any sort of horror and vice. . . . Pure spirit is pure falsehood. . . . As long as the priest, the *professional* denier, calumniator and poisoner of life, is considered as the *highest* kind of man, there can be no answer to the question, what *is* truth? Truth has already been turned topsy-turvy, when the conscious advocate of nonentity and of denial passes as the representative of "truth."

9

It is upon this theological instinct that I wage war. I find traces of it everywhere. Whoever has the blood of theologians in his veins, stands from the start in a false and dishonest position to all things. The pathos which grows out of this state, is called *Faith:* that is to say, to shut one's eyes once and for all, in order not to suffer at the sight of incurable falsity. People convert this faulty view of all things into a moral, a virtue, a thing of holiness. They endow their distorted vision with a good conscience,—they claim that no *other* point of view is any longer of value, once theirs has been made sacrosanct with the names "God," "Salvation," "Eternity." I unearthed the instinct of the theologian everywhere : it is the most universal, and actually the most subterranean form of falsity on earth. That which a theologian considers true, *must* of necessity be false : this furnishes almost the criterion of truth. It is his most profound self-preservative instinct which forbids reality ever to attain to honour in any way, or even to raise its voice. Whithersoever the influence of the theologian extends, *valuations* are topsy-turvy, and the concepts "true" and "false" have necessarily changed places : that which is most deleterious to life, is here called "true," that which enhances it, elevates it, says Yea to it, justifies it and renders it triumphant, is called "false." . . . If it should happen that theologians, *via* the "conscience" either of princes or of the people, stretch out their hand for power, let us not be in any doubt as to what results therefrom each time, namely :—the will to the end, the *nihilistic* will to power. . . .

10

Among Germans I am immediately understood when I say, that philosophy is ruined by the blood of theologians. The Protestant minister is the grandfather of German philosophy, Protestantism itself is the latter's *peccatum originale.* Definition of Protestantism : the partial paralysis of Christianity — and of reason. . . . One needs only to pronounce the words "Tübingen Seminary," in order to understand what German philosophy really is at bottom, *i.e.:*—

theology *in disguise*. . . . The Swabians are the
best liars in Germany, they lie innocently. . . .
Whence came all the rejoicing with which the
appearance of Kant was greeted by the scholastic
world of Germany, three-quarters of which consist
of clergymen's and schoolmasters' sons? Whence
came the German conviction, which finds an echo
even now, that Kant inaugurated a change for the
better? The theologian's instinct in the German
scholar divined what had once again been made
possible. . . . A back-staircase leading into the old
ideal was discovered, the concept "true world," the
concept morality as the *essence* of the world (—those
two most vicious errors that have ever existed!), were,
thanks to a subtle and wily scepticism, once again,
if not demonstrable, at least no longer *refutable*. . . .
Reason, the *prerogative* of reason, does not extend
so far. . . Out of reality they had made "appearance"; and an absolutely false world—that of being
—had been declared to be reality. Kant's success
is merely a theologian's success. Like Luther, and
like Leibniz, Kant was one brake the more upon
the already squeaky wheel of German uprightness.

II

One word more against Kant as a *moralist.* A
virtue *must* be *our* invention, our most personal
defence and need: in every other sense it is merely
a danger. That which does not constitute a condition of our life, is merely harmful to it: to possess
a virtue merely because one happens to respect the
concept "virtue," as Kant would have us do, is pernicious. "Virtue," "Duty," "Goodness in itself."

goodness stamped with the character of imperson-
ality and universal validity—these things are mere
mental hallucinations, in which decline the final
devitalisation of life and Kœnigsbergian Chinadom
find expression. The most fundamental laws of preservation and growth, demand precisely the reverse,
namely :—that each should discover *his* own virtue,
his own Categorical Imperative. A nation goes to
the dogs when it confounds its concept of duty with
the general concept of duty. Nothing is more profoundly, more thoroughly pernicious, than every
impersonal feeling of duty, than every sacrifice to
the Moloch of abstraction.—Fancy no one's having
thought Kant's Categorical Imperative *dangerous to
life !* . . . The instinct of the theologist alone took
it under its wing!—An action stimulated by the
instinct of life, is proved to be a proper action by
the happiness that accompanies it : and that nihilist
with the bowels of a Christian dogmatist regarded
happiness as an *objection.* . . . What is there that
destroys a man more speedily than to work, think,
feel, as an automaton of "duty," without internal
promptings, without a profound personal predilection, without joy? This is the recipe *par excellence*
of decadence and even of idiocy. . . . Kant became
an idiot.—And he was the contemporary of Goethe!
This fatal spider was regarded as *the* German philosopher, — is still regarded as such! . . . I refrain
from saying what I think of the Germans. . . . Did
Kant not see in the French Revolution the transi-
tion of the State from the inorganic to the *organic*
form ? Did he not ask himself whether there was
a single event on record which could be explained

otherwise than as a moral faculty of mankind ; so that by means of it, " mankind's tendency towards good," might be *proved* once and for all ? Kant's reply : " that is the Revolution." Instinct at fault in anything and everything, hostility to nature as an instinct, German decadence made into philosophy —*that is Kant!*

12

Except for a few sceptics, the respectable type in the history of philosophy, the rest do not know the very first pre-requisite of intellectual upright-ness. They all behave like females, do these great enthusiasts and animal prodigies, — they regard " beautiful feelings " themselves as arguments, the " heaving breast " as the bellows of divinity, and conviction as the *criterion* of truth. In the end, even Kant, with " Teutonic " innocence, tried to dress this lack of intellectual conscience up in a scientific garb by means of the concept " practical reason." He deliberately invented a kind of reason which at times would allow one to dispense with reason, that is to say when " morality," when the sublime command " thou shalt," makes itself heard. When one remembers that in almost all nations the philosopher is only a further development of the priestly type, this heirloom of priesthood, this *fraud towards one's self,* no longer surprises one. When a man has a holy life-task, as for instance to im-prove, save, or deliver mankind, when a man bears God in his breast, and is the mouthpiece of impera-tives from another world,—with such a mission he stands beyond the pale of all merely reasonable valuations. He is even sanctified by such a taste,

and is already the type of a higher order! What
does a priest care about science! He stands too
high for that!—And until now the priest has *ruled!*
—He it was who determined the concept "true
and false."

13

Do not let us undervalue the fact that we *ourselves*, we free spirits, are already a "transvaluation
of all values," an incarnate declaration of war
against all the old concepts "true" and "untrue"
and of a triumph over them. The most valuable
standpoints are always the last to be found: but the
most valuable standpoints are the methods. All
the methods and the first principles of our modern
scientific procedure, had for years to encounter the
profoundest contempt: association with them meant
exclusion from the society of decent people—one
was regarded as an "enemy of God," as a scoffer
at truth and as "one possessed." With one's
scientific nature, one belonged to the Chandala.
We have had the whole feeling of mankind against
us; hitherto their notion of that which ought to be
truth, of that which ought to serve the purpose
of truth: every "thou shalt," has been directed
against us. . . . Our objects, our practices, our calm,
cautious distrustful manner—everything about us
seemed to them absolutely despicable and beneath
contempt. After all, it might be asked with some
justice, whether the thing which kept mankind
blindfold so long, were not an æsthetic taste: what
they demanded of truth was a *picturesque* effect,
and from the man of science what they expected
was that he should make a forcible appeal to their

senses.   It was our *modesty* which ran counter to
their taste so long. . .   And oh! how well they
guessed this, did these divine turkey-cocks!—

14

We have altered our standpoint.   In every respect
we have become more modest.   We no longer derive
man from the "spirit," and from the "godhead";
we have thrust him back among the beasts.   We
regard him as the strongest animal, because he is
the craftiest: one of the results thereof is his intellectuality.   On the other hand we guard against
the vain pretension, which even here would fain
assert itself: that man is the great *arrière pensée* of
organic evolution!   He is by no means the crown
of creation, beside him, every other creature stands
at the same stage of perfection. . . . And even in
asserting this we go a little too far; for, relatively
speaking, man is the most botched and diseased of
animals, and he has wandered furthest from his
instincts.   Be all this as it may, he is certainly the
most *interesting!*   As regards animals, Descartes
was the first, with really admirable daring, to venture
the thought that the beast was *machina*, and the
whole of our physiology is endeavouring to prove
this proposition.   Moreover, logically we do not set
man apart, as Descartes did: the extent to which
man is understood to-day goes only so far as he
has been understood mechanistically.   Formerly man
was given "free will," as his dowry from a higher
sphere; nowadays we have robbed him even of will,
in view of the fact that no such faculty is any longer
known.   The only purpose served by the old word

"will," is to designate a result, a sort of individual reaction which necessarily follows upon a host of partly discordant and partly harmonious stimuli :— the will no longer "effects " or "moves" anything. . . . Formerly people thought that man's consciousness, his " spirit," was a proof of his lofty origin, of his divinity. With the idea of perfecting man, he was conjured to draw his senses inside himself, after the manner of the tortoise, to cut off all relations with terrestrial things, and to divest himself of his mortal shell. Then the most important thing about him, the " pure spirit," would remain over. Even concerning these things we have improved our standpoint. Consciousness, " spirit," now seems to us rather a symptom of relative imperfection in the organism, as an experiment, a groping, a misapprehension, an affliction which absorbs an unnecessary quantity of nervous energy. We deny that anything can be done perfectly so long as it is done consciously. " Pure spirit " is a piece of " pure stupidity " : if we discount the nervous system, the senses and the "mortal shell," we have miscalculated —that it is all ! . . .

15

In Christianity, neither morality nor religion comes in touch at all with reality. Nothing but imaginary *causes* (God, the soul, the ego, spirit, free will — or even non-free will); nothing but imaginary *effects* (sin, salvation, grace, punishment, forgiveness of sins). Imaginary beings are supposed to have intercourse (God, spirits, souls); imaginary Natural History (anthropocentric : total lack of the notion " natural causes "); an imaginary *psychology* (nothing

but misunderstandings of self, interpretations of
pleasant or unpleasant general feelings; for instance
of the states of the *nervus sympathicus*, with the help
of the sign language of a religio-moral idiosyncrasy,
—repentance, pangs of conscience, the temptation of
the devil, the presence of God); an imaginary tele-
ology (the Kingdom of God, the Last Judgment,
Everlasting Life).—This purely fictitious world distinguishes itself very unfavourably from the world
of dreams : the latter *reflects* reality, whereas the
former falsifies, depreciates and denies it. Once the
concept "nature" was taken to mean the opposite
of the concept God, the word "natural" had to
acquire the meaning of abominable,—the whole of
that fictitious world takes its root in the hatred of
nature (—reality!—),it is the expression of profound
discomfiture in the presence of reality. . . . *But
this explains everything.* What is the only kind
of man who has reasons for wriggling out of reality
by lies? The man who suffers from reality. But
in order to suffer from reality one must be a bungled
portion of it. The preponderance of pain over
pleasure is the *cause* of that fictitious morality and
religion : but any such preponderance furnishes the
formula for decadence.

16

A criticism of the Christian concept of God inevit-
ably leads to the same conclusion.—A nation that
still believes in itself, also has its own God. In him
it honours the conditions which enable it to remain
uppermost,—that is to say, its virtues. It projects
its joy over itself, its feeling of power, into a being, to

whom it can be thankful for such things. He who is rich, will give of his riches: a proud people requires a God, unto whom it can *sacrifice* things. . . . Religion, when restricted to these principles, is a form of gratitude. A man is grateful for his own existence; for this he must have a God.—Such a God must be able to benefit and to injure him, he must be able to act the friend and the foe. He must be esteemed for his good as well as for his evil qualities. The monstrous castration of a God by making him a God only of goodness, would lie beyond the pale of the desires of such a community. The evil God is just as urgently needed as the good God: for a people in such a form of society certainly does not owe its existence to toleration and humaneness. . . . What would be the good of a God who knew nothing of anger, revenge, envy, scorn, craft, and violence? —who had perhaps never experienced the rapturous *ardeurs* of victory and of annihilation? No one would understand such a God: why should one possess him?—Of course, when a people is on the road to ruin; when it feels its belief in a future, its hope of freedom vanishing for ever; when it becomes conscious of submission as the most useful quality, and of the virtues of the submissive as self-preservative measures, then its God must also modify himself. He then becomes a tremulous and unassuming sneak; he counsels " peace of the soul," the cessation of all hatred, leniency and " love " even towards friend and foe. He is for ever moralising, he crawls into the heart of every private virtue, becomes a God for everybody, he retires from active service and becomes a Cosmopolitan. . . . Formerly he repre-

sented a people, the strength of a people, everything
aggressive and desirous of power lying concealed in
the heart of a nation : now he is merely the good
God. . . . In very truth Gods have no other alternative, they are *either* the Will to Power—in which
case they are always the Gods of whole nations,—
or, on the other hand, the incapacity for power — in
which case they necessarily become good.

17

Wherever the Will to Power, no matter in what
form, begins to decline, a physiological retrogression,
decadence, always supervenes.   The godhead of
decadence, shorn of its masculine virtues and passions
is perforce converted into the God of the physiologi-
cally degraded, of the weak.   Of course they do not
call themselves the weak, they call themselves "the
good." . . . No hint will be necessary to help you
to understand at what moment in history the dual-
istic fiction of a good and an evil God first became
possible.   With the same instinct by which the
subjugated reduce their God to "Goodness in itself,"
they also cancel the good qualities from their con-
querer's God; they avenge themselves on their
masters by diabolising the latter's God.—The *good
God* and the devil as well :—both the abortions
of decadence.—How is it possible that we are still
so indulgent towards the simplicity of Christian
theologians to-day, as to declare with them that the
evolution of the concept God, from the "God of
Israel," the God of a people, to the Christian God,
the quintessence of all goodness, marks a *step forward* ?—But even Renan does this.   As if Renan

had a right to simplicity! Why the very contrary stares one in the face. When the pre-requisites of *ascending* life, when everything strong, plucky, masterful and proud has been eliminated from the concept of God, and step by step he has sunk down to the symbol of a staff for the weary, of a last straw for all those who are drowning; when he becomes the pauper's God, the sinner's God, the sick man's God *par excellence*, and the attribute "Saviour," "Redeemer," remains *over* as the one essential attribute of divinity: what does such a metamorphosis, such an abasement of the godhead imply?—Undoubtedly, "the kingdom of God" has thus become larger. Formerly all he had was his people, his "chosen" people. Since then he has gone travelling over foreign lands, just as his people have done; since then he has never rested anywhere: until one day he felt at home everywhere, the Great Cosmopolitan,—until he got the "greatest number," and half the world on his side. But the God of the "greatest number," the democrat among gods, did not become a proud heathen god notwithstanding: he remained a Jew, he remained the God of the back streets, the God of all dark corners and hovels, of all the unwholesome quarters of the world! . . . His universal empire is now as ever a netherworld empire, an infirmary, a subterranean empire, a ghetto-empire. . . . And he himself is so pale, so weak, so decadent. . . . Even the palest of the pale were able to master him—our friends the metaphysicians, those albinos of thought. They spun their webs around him so long that ultimately he was hypnotised by their movements and himself became a spider, a metaphysician. Thenceforward he once more began spinning the world out of his inner being—*sub specie Spinozæ*,—thenceforward he transfigured himself into something ever thinner and ever more anæmic, became "ideal," became "pure spirit," became *"absolutum,"* and "thing-in-itself." . . . *The decline and fall of a god:* God became the "thing-in-itself."

18

The Christian concept of God—God as the deity of the sick, God as a spider, God as spirit—is one of the most corrupt concepts of God that has ever been attained on earth. Maybe it represents the low-water mark in the evolutionary ebb of the godlike type. God degenerated into the *contradiction of life*, instead of being its transfiguration and eternal Yea! With God war is declared on life, nature, and the will to life! God is the formula for every calumny of this world and for every lie concerning a beyond! In God, nonentity is deified, and the will to nonentity is declared holy!

19

The fact that the strong races of Northern Europe did not repudiate the Christian God, certainly does not do any credit to their religious power, not to speak of their taste. They ought to have been able successfully to cope with such a morbid and decrepit offshoot of decadence. And a curse lies on their heads ; because they were unable to cope with him : they made illness, decrepitude and contradiction a part of all their instincts,—since then they have not

created any other God ! Two thousand years have
passed and not a single new God ! But still there
exists, and as if by right,—like an *ultimum* and
maximum of god-creating power,—the *creator spiri-
tus* in man, this miserable God of Christian mono-
tono-theism ! This hybrid creature of decay, nonentity, concept and contradiction, in which all the
instincts of decadence, all the cowardices and lan-
guors of the soul find their sanction !— —

20

With my condemnation of Christianity I should
not like to have done an injustice to a religion which
is related to it and the number of whose followers
is even greater ; I refer to Buddhism. As nihilistic
religions, they are akin, — they are religions of
decadence,—while each is separated from the other
in the most extraordinary fashion. For being able
to compare them at all, the critic of Christianity is
profoundly grateful to Indian scholars.—Buddhism
is a hundred times more realistic than Christianity,
—it is part of its constitutional heritage to be able
to face problems objectively and coolly, it is the outcome of centuries of lasting philosophical activity.
The concept " God " was already exploded when it
appeared. Buddhism is the only really *positive*
religion to be found in history, even in its epis-
temology (which is strict phenomenalism)—it no
longer speaks of the " struggle with *sin*," but fully
recognising the true nature of reality it speaks of
the " struggle with *pain*." It already has—and this
distinguishes it fundamentally from Christianity,—
the self-deception of moral concepts beneath it,—to

use my own phraseology, it stands *Beyond Good and Evil.* The two physiological facts upon which it rests and upon which it bestows its attention are: in the first place excessive irritability of feeling, which manifests itself as a refined susceptibility to pain, *and also* as super-spiritualisation, an all-too-lengthy sojourn amid concepts and logical procedures, under the influence of which the personal instinct has suffered in favour of the "impersonal." (—Both of these states will be known to a few of my readers, the objective ones, who, like myself, will know them from experience.) Thanks to these physiological conditions, a state of depression set in, which Buddha sought to combat by means of hygiene. Against it, he prescribes life in the open, a life of travel; moderation and careful choice in food; caution in regard to all intoxicating liquor, as also in regard to all the passions which tend to create bile and to heat the blood; and he deprecates care either on one's own or on other people's account. He recommends ideas that bring one either peace or good cheer,—he invents means whereby the habit of contrary ideas may be lost. He understands goodness —being good—as promoting health. *Prayer* is out of the question, as is also *asceticism;* there is neither a Categorical Imperative nor any discipline whatsoever, even within the walls of a monastery (—it is always possible to leave it if one wants to). All these things would have been only a means of accentuating the excessive irritability already referred to. Precisely on this account he does not exhort his followers to wage war upon those who do not share their views; nothing is more abhorred in his doctrine than the feeling of revenge, of aversion, and of resentment (—"not through hostility doth hostility end": the touching refrain of the whole of Buddhism . . .). And in this he was right; for it is precisely these passions which are thoroughly unhealthy in view of the principal dietetic object. The mental fatigue which he finds already existent and which expresses itself in excessive "objectivity" (*i.e.*, the enfeeblement of the individual's interest—loss of ballast and of "egoism"), he combats by leading the spiritual interests as well imperatively back to the individual. In Buddha's doctrine egoism is a duty: the thing which is above all necessary, *i.e.*, "how canst thou be rid of suffering" regulates and defines the whole of the spiritual diet (—let anyone but think of that Athenian who also declared war upon pure "scientificality," Socrates, who made a morality out of personal egoism even in the realm of problems).

21

The pre-requisites for Buddhism are a very mild climate, great gentleness and liberality in the customs of a people and *no* militarism. The movement must also originate among the higher and even learned classes. Cheerfulness, peace and absence of desire, are the highest of inspirations, and they are *realised*. Buddhism is not a religion in which perfection is merely aspired to : perfection is the normal case. In Christianity all the instincts of the subjugated and oppressed come to the fore : it is the lowest classes who seek their salvation in this religion. Here the pastime, the manner of

killing time is to practise the casuistry of sin, self-
criticism, and conscience inquisition.   Here the
ecstasy in the presence of a *powerful being*, called
" god," is constantly maintained by means of
prayer ; while the highest thing is regarded as un-
attainable, as a gift, as an act of " grace."   Here
plain dealing is also entirely lacking : concealment
and the darkened room are Christian.   Here the
body is despised, hygiene is repudiated as sensual ;
the church repudiates even cleanliness (—the first
Christian measure after the banishment of the
Moors was the closing of the public baths, of which
Cordova alone possessed 270).   A certain spirit of
cruelty towards one's self and others is also Christian :
hatred of all those who do not share one's views ;
the will to persecute.   Sombre and exciting ideas
are in the foreground ; the most coveted states and
those which are endowed with the finest names, are
really epileptic in their nature ; diet is selected in
such a way as to favour morbid symptoms and
to over-excite the nerves.   Christian, too, is the
mortal hatred of the earth's rulers,—the " noble,"—
and at the same time a sort of concealed and secret
competition with them (the subjugated leave the
" body" to their master—all they want is the
" soul ").   Christian is the hatred of the intellect, of
pride, of courage, freedom, intellectual *libertinage ;*
Christian is the hatred of the *senses*, of the joys of
the senses, of joy in general.

22

When Christianity departed from its native soil,
which consisted of the lowest classes, the *submerged*

masses of the ancient world, and set forth in quest of power among barbaric nations, it no longer met with exhausted men but inwardly savage and self-lacerating men — the strong but bungled men. Here, dissatisfaction with one's self, suffering through one's self, is not as in the case of Buddhism, excessive irritability and susceptibility to pain, but rather, conversely, it is an inordinate desire for inflicting pain, for a discharge of the inner tension in hostile deeds and ideas. Christianity was in need of *barbaric* ideas and values, in order to be able to master barbarians : such are for instance, the sacrifice of the first-born, the drinking of blood at communion, the contempt of the intellect and of culture ; torture in all its forms, sensual and non-sensual ; the great pomp of the cult. Buddhism is a religion for *senile* men, for races which have become kind, gentle, and over-spiritual, and which feel pain too easily (—Europe is not nearly ripe for it yet—) ; it calls them back to peace and cheerfulness, to a regimen for the intellect, to a certain hardening of the body. Christianity aims at mastering *beasts of prey ;* its expedient is to make them *ill,*—to render feeble is the Christian recipe for taming, for " civilisation." Buddhism is a religion for the close and exhaustion of civilisation ; Christianity does not even find civilisation at hand when it appears, in certain circumstances it lays the foundation of civilisation.

23

Buddhism, I repeat, is a hundred times colder, more truthful, more objective. It no longer requires

to justify pain and its susceptibility to suffering by
the interpretation of sin,—it simply says what it
thinks, " I suffer." To the barbarian, on the other
hand, suffering in itself is not a respectable thing :
in order to acknowledge to himself that he suffers,
what he requires, in the first place, is an explanation
(his instinct directs him more readily to deny his
suffering, or to endure it in silence). In his case,
the word "devil" was a blessing : man had an
almighty and terrible enemy,—he had no reason to
be ashamed of suffering at the hands of such an
enemy.—

At bottom there are in Christianity one or two
subtleties which belong to the Orient. In the first
place it knows that it is a matter of indifference
whether a thing be true or not; but that it is of the
highest importance that it should be believed to be
true. Truth and the belief that something is true :
two totally separate worlds of interest, almost
opposite worlds, the road to the one and the road to
the other lie absolutely apart. To be initiated into
this fact almost constitutes one a sage in the Orient :
the Brahmins understood it thus, so did Plato, and
so does every disciple of esoteric wisdom. If for
example it give anyone pleasure to believe himself
delivered from sin, it is *not* a necessary prerequisite
thereto that he should be sinful, but only that he
should *feel* sinful. If, however, *faith* is above all
necessary, then reason, knowledge, and scientific
research must be brought into evil repute : the road
to truth becomes the *forbidden* road.—Strong *hope*
is a much greater stimulant of life than any single
realised joy could be. Sufferers must be sustained

by a hope which no actuality can contradict,—and which cannot ever be realised : the hope of another world. (Precisely on account of this power that hope has of making the unhappy linger on, the Greeks regarded it as the evil of evils, as the most *mischievous* evil : it remained behind in Pandora's box.) In order that *love* may be possible, God must be a person. In order that the lowest instincts may also make their voices heard God must be young. For the ardour of the women a beautiful saint, and for the ardour of the men a Virgin Mary has to be pressed into the foreground. All this on condition that Christianity wishes to rule over a certain soil, on which Aphrodisiac or Adonis cults had already determined the *notion* of a cult. To insist upon *chastity* only intensifies the vehemence and pro-fundity of the religious instinct — it makes the cult warmer, more enthusiastic, more soulful.—Love is the state in which man sees things most widely different from what they are. The force of illusion reaches its zenith here, as likewise the sweetening and transfiguring power. When a man is in love he endures more than at other times ; he submits to everything. The thing was to discover a religion in which it was possible to love : by this means the worst in life is overcome—it is no longer even seen. —So much for three Christian virtues Faith, Hope, and Charity : I call them the three Christian *precau-tionary measures.*—Buddhism is too full of aged wisdom, too positivistic to be shrewd in this way.

24

Here I only touch upon the problem of the origin

of Christianity. The first principle of its solution reads : Christianity can be understood only in relation to the soil out of which it grew,—it is not a counter-movement against the Jewish instinct, it is the rational outcome of the latter, one step further in its appalling logic. In the formula of the Saviour: " for Salvation is of the Jews."—The second principle is : the psychological type of the Galilean is still recognisable, but it was only in a state of utter degeneration (which is at once a distortion and an overloading with foreign features) that he was able to serve the purpose for which he has been used,— namely, as the type of a Redeemer of mankind.

The Jews are the most remarkable people in the history of the world, because when they were confronted with the question of Being or non-Being, with simply uncanny deliberateness, they preferred Being *at any price :* this price was the fundamental *falsification* of all Nature, all the naturalness and all the reality, of the inner quite as much as of the outer world. They hedged themselves in behind all those conditions under which hitherto a people has been able to live, has been allowed to live ; of themselves they created an idea which was the reverse of *natural* conditions,—each in turn, they twisted first religion, then the cult, then morality, history and psychology, about in a manner so perfectly hopeless that they were made *to contradict their natural value.* We meet with the same phenomena again, and exaggerated to an incalculable degree, although only as a copy :—the Christian Church as compared with the " chosen people," lacks all claim to originality. Precisely on this account the Jews are the most *fatal*

people in the history of the world : their ultimate
influence has falsified mankind to such an extent,
that even to this day the Christian can be anti-
Semitic in spirit, without comprehending that he
himself is the *final consequence of Judaism.*

It was in my " Genealogy of Morals " that I first
gave a psychological exposition of the idea of the
antithesis noble- and *resentment*-morality, the latter
having arisen out of an attitude of negation to the
former : but this is Judæo-Christian morality heart
and soul.   In order to be able to say Nay to everything that represents the ascending movement of
life, prosperity, power, beauty, and self-affirmation
on earth, the instinct of resentment, become genius,
had to invent *another* world, from the standpoint
of which that *Yea-saying* to life appeared as *the*
most evil and most abominable thing.   From the
psychological standpoint the Jewish people are possessed of the toughest vitality.   Transplanted amid
impossible conditions, with profound self-preservative intelligence, it voluntarily took the side of all
the instincts of decadence,—*not* as though dominated by them, but because it detected a power in
them by means of which it could assert itself *against*
" the world."   The Jews are the opposite of all *decadents :* they have been forced to represent them
to the point of illusion, and with a *non plus ultra* of
histrionic genius, they have known how to set themselves at the head of all decadent movements (St
Paul and Christianity for instance), in order to create
something from them which is stronger than every
party *saying Yea to life.*   For the category of men
which aspires to power in Judaism and Christianity,

—that is to say, for the sacerdotal class, decadence is but a *means:* this category of men has a vital interest in making men sick, and in turning the notions "good" and "bad," " true" and "false," upside down in a manner which is not only dangerous to life, but also slanders it.

25

The history of Israel is invaluable as the typical history of every *denaturalisation* of natural values : let me point to five facts which relate thereto. Originally, and above all in the period of the kings, even Israel's attitude to all things was the *right* one —that is to say, the natural one. Its Jehovah was the expression of its consciousness of power, of its joy over itself, of its hope for itself: victory and salvation were expected from him, through him it was confident that Nature would give what a people requires—above all rain. Jehovah is the God of Israel, and *consequently* the God of justice : this is the reasoning of every people which is in the position of power, and which has a good conscience in that position. In the solemn cult both sides of this self-affirmation of a people find expression : it is grateful for the great strokes of fate by means of which it became uppermost ; it is grateful for the regularity in the succession of the seasons and for all good fortune in the rearing of cattle and in the tilling of the soil.—This state of affairs remained the ideal for some considerable time, even after it had been swept away in a deplorable manner by anarchy from within and the Assyrians from without. But the people still retained, as their highest desideratum, that vision

of a king who was a good soldier and a severe judge;
and he who retained it most of all was that typical
prophet (—that is to say, critic and satirist of the
age), Isaiah.—But all hopes remained unrealised.
The old God was no longer able to do what he had
done formerly. He ought to have been dropped.
What happened? The idea of him was changed,—
the idea of him was denaturalised : this was the price
they paid for retaining him.—Jehovah, the God of
" Justice,"—is no longer one with Israel, no longer
the expression of a people's sense of dignity : he is
only a god on certain conditions. . . . The idea of
him becomes a weapon in the hands of priestly
agitators who henceforth interpret all happiness as
a reward, all unhappiness as a punishment for disobedience to God, for " sin " : that most fraudulent
method of interpretation which arrives at a so-called
" moral order of the Universe," by means of which
the concept " cause " and " effect " is turned upside
down. Once natural causation has been swept out
of the world by reward and punishment, a causation
hostile to nature becomes necessary ; whereupon all the
forms of unnaturalness follow. A God who *demands*,
—in the place of a God who helps, who advises, who
is at bottom only a name for every happy inspiration
of courage and of self-reliance. . . . Morality is no
longer the expression of the conditions of life and
growth, no longer the most fundamental instinct of
life, but it has become abstract, it has become the
opposite of life,—Morality as the fundamental perversion of the imagination, as the " evil eye " for all
things. What is Jewish morality, what is Christian
morality? Chance robbed of its innocence; unhappi-

ness polluted with the idea of "sin"; well-being
interpreted as a danger, as a "temptation"; physiological indisposition poisoned by means of the canker-
worm of conscience. . . .

26

The concept of God falsified; the concept of
morality falsified : but the Jewish priesthood did
not stop at this.   No use could be made of the
whole *history* of Israel, therefore it must go !   These
priests accomplished that miracle of falsification, of
which the greater part of the Bible is the document :
with unparalleled contempt and in the teeth of all
tradition and historical facts, they interpreted their
own people's past in a religious manner,—that is to
say, they converted it into a ridiculous mechanical
process of salvation, on the principle that all sin
against Jehovah led to punishment, and that all pious
worship of Jehovah led to reward.   We would feel this
shameful act of historical falsification far more poig-
nantly if the ecclesiastical interpretation of history
through millenniums had not blunted almost all our
sense for the demands of uprightness *in historicis*.
And the church is seconded by the philosophers :
the lie of "a moral order of the universe" per-
meates the whole development even of more modern
philosophy.   What does a "moral order of the universe" mean ?   That once and for all there is such
a thing as a will of God which determines what man
has to do and what he has to leave undone ; that the
value of a people or of an individual is measured
according to how much or how little the one or the
other obeys the will of God ; that in the destinies

of a people or of an individual, the will of God
shows itself dominant, that is to say it punishes or
rewards according to the degree of obedience.   In
the place of this miserable falsehood, *reality* says : a
parasitical type of man, who can flourish only
at the cost of all the healthy elements of life, the
priest abuses the name of God : he calls that state
of affairs in which the priest determines the value of
things " the Kingdom of God " ; he calls the means
whereby such a state of affairs is attained or maintained, " the Will of God " ; with cold-blooded
cynicism he measures peoples, ages and individuals
according to whether they favour or oppose the
ascendancy of the priesthood.   Watch him at work :
in the hands of the Jewish priesthood the Augustan
Age in the history of Israel became an age of
decline ; the exile, the protracted misfortune trans-
formed itself into eternal *punishment* for the
Augustan Age—that age in which the priest did
not yet exist.   Out of the mighty and thoroughly
free-born figures of the history of Israel, they made,
according to their requirements, either wretched
bigots and hypocrites, or " godless ones " : they
simplified the psychology of every great event to
the idiotic formula " obedient or disobedient to
God."—A step further : the " Will of God," that is
to say the self-preservative measures of the priesthood, must be known—to this end a " revelation "
is necessary.   In plain English : a stupendous literary fraud becomes necessary, " holy scriptures " are
discovered,—and they are published abroad with all
hieratic pomp, with days of penance and lamenta-
tions over the long state of " sin."   The " Will of

God" has long stood firm : the whole of the trouble lies in the fact that the "Holy Scriptures" have been discarded. . . . Moses was already the "Will of God" revealed. . . . What had happened? With severity and pedantry, the priest had formulated once and for all—even to the largest and smallest contributions that were to be paid to him (—not forgetting the daintiest portions of meat; for the priest is a consumer of beef-steaks)—*what he wanted*, "what the Will of God was." . . . Henceforward everything became so arranged that the priests were *indispensable everywhere.* At all the natural events of life, at birth, at marriage, at the sick-bed, at death,—not to speak of the sacrifice ("the meal"),—the holy parasite appears in order to denaturalise, or in his language, to "sanctify," everything. . . . For this should be understood : every natural custom, every natural institution (the State, the administration of justice, marriage, the care of the sick and the poor), every demand inspired by the instinct of life, in short everything that has a value in itself, is rendered absolutely worthless and even dangerous through the parasitism of the priest (or of the "moral order of the universe") : a sanction after the fact is required,—a *power which imparts value* is necessary, which in so doing says, Nay to nature, and which by this means alone *creates* a valuation. . . . The priest depreciates and desecrates nature : it is only at this price that he exists at all.—Disobedience to God, that is to say, to the priest, to the "law," now receives the name of "sin"; the means of "reconciling one's self with God" are of course of a nature which

render subordination to the priesthood all the more
fundamental: the priest alone is able to "save." ...
From the psychological standpoint, in every society
organised upon a hieratic basis, "sins" are indispensable: they are the actual weapons of power,
the priest *lives* upon sins, it is necessary for him
that people should "sin." . . . Supreme axiom:
"God forgiveth him that repenteth"—in plain
English: *him that submitteth himself to the priest.*

27

Christianity grew out of an utterly *false* soil, in
which all nature, every natural value, every *reality*
had the deepest instincts of the ruling class against
it; it was a form of deadly hostility to reality which
has never been surpassed. The "holy people" which
had retained only priestly values and priestly names
for all things, and which, with a logical consistency
that is terrifying, had divorced itself from everything still powerful on earth as if it were " unholy,"
" worldly," " sinful,"—this people created a final
formula for its instinct which was consistent to the
point of self-suppression ; as *Christianity* it denied
even the last form of reality, the " holy people," the
" chosen people," *Jewish* reality itself. The case is
of supreme interest: the small insurrectionary movement christened with the name of Jesus of Nazareth,
is the Jewish instinct *over again*, — in other words,
it is the sacerdotal instinct which can no longer
endure the priest as a fact; it is the discovery of a
kind of life even more fantastic than the one previously conceived, a vision of life which is even
more unreal than that which the organisation

of a church stipulates. Christianity denies the church.*

I fail to see against whom was directed the insurrection of which rightly or *wrongly* Jesus is understood to have been the promoter, if it were not directed against the Jewish church, — the word "church" being used here in precisely the same sense in which it is used to-day. It was an insurrection against the "good and the just," against the "prophets of Israel," against the hierarchy of society —not against the latter's corruption, but against caste, privilege, order, formality. It was the lack of faith in "higher men," it was a "Nay" uttered against everything that was tinctured with the blood of priests and theologians. But the hierarchy which was set in question if only temporarily by this movement, formed the construction of piles upon which, alone, the Jewish people was able to subsist in the midst of the "waters"; it was that people's *last* chance of survival wrested from the world at enormous pains, the *residuum* of its political autonomy: to attack this construction was tantamount to attacking the most profound popular instinct, the most tenacious national will to live that has ever existed on earth. This saintly anarchist who called the lowest of the low, the outcasts and "sinners," the Chandala of Judaism, to revolt against the established order of things (and in

---

* It will be seen from this that in spite of Nietzsche's ruthless criticism of the priests, he draws a sharp distinction between Christianity and the Church. As the latter still contained elements of order, it was more to his taste than the denial of authority characteristic of real Christianity.—TR.

language which, if the gospels are to be trusted, would get one sent to Siberia even to-day)—this man was a political criminal in so far as political criminals were possible in a community so absurdly non-political. This brought him to the cross : the proof of this is the inscription found thereon. He died for *his* sins — and no matter how often the contrary has been asserted there is absolutely nothing to show that he died for the sins of others.

28

As to whether he was conscious of this contrast, or whether he was merely *regarded* as such, is quite another question. And here, alone, do I touch upon the problem of the psychology of the Saviour.—I confess there are few books which I have as much difficulty in reading as the gospels. These difficulties are quite different from those which allowed the learned curiosity of the German mind to celebrate one of its most memorable triumphs. Many years have now elapsed since I, like every young scholar, with the sage conscientiousness of a refined philologist, relished the work of the incomparable Strauss. I was then twenty years of age ; now I am too serious for that sort of thing. What do I care about the contradictions of "tradition" ? How can saintly legends be called " tradition " at all ! The stories of saints constitute the most ambiguous literature on earth : to apply the scientific method to them, *when there are no other documents to hand*, seems to me to be a fatal procedure from the start —simply learned fooling.

29

The point that concerns me is the psychological
type of the Saviour.   This type might be contained
in the gospels, in spite of the gospels, and however
much it may have been mutilated, or overladen with
foreign features : just as that of Francis of Assisi is
contained in his legends in spite of his legends.   It
is *not* a question of the truth concerning what he has
done, what he has said, and how he actually died ;
but whether his type may still be conceived in any
way, whether it has been handed down to us at all ?
—The attempts which to my knowledge have been
made to read the *history* of a " soul " out of the
gospels, seem to me to point only to disreputable
levity in psychological matters.   M. Renan, that
buffoon *in psychologicis*, has contributed the two
most monstrous ideas imaginable to the explanation of the type of Jesus : the idea of the *genius* and
the idea of the *hero* (" *héros* ").   But if there is anything thoroughly unevangelical surely it is the idea
of the hero.   It is precisely the reverse of all struggle,
of all consciousness of taking part in the fight, that
has become instinctive here : the inability to resist
is here converted into a morality (" resist not evil,"
the profoundest sentence in the whole of the gospels,
their key in a certain sense), the blessedness of peace,
of gentleness, of not *being able* to be an enemy.   What
is the meaning of "glad tidings" ?—True life, eternal
life has been found—it is not promised, it is actually
here, it is in *you ;* it is life in love, in love free from
all selection or exclusion, free from all distance.
Everybody is the child of God—Jesus does not by

any means claim anything for himself alone,—as
the child of God everybody is equal to everybody
else. . . . Fancy making Jesus a *hero !*—And what
a tremendous misunderstanding the word "genius"
is ! Our whole idea of "spirit," which is a civilised
idea, could have had no meaning whatever in the
world in which Jesus lived. In the strict terms of
the physiologist, a very different word ought to be
used here. . . . We know of a condition of morbid
irritability of the sense of *touch*, which recoils shud-
dering from every kind of contact, and from every
attempt at grasping a solid object. Any such physiological *habitus* reduced to its ultimate logical conclusion, becomes an instinctive hatred of all reality, a
flight into the "intangible," into the "incomprehens-
ible"; a repugnance to all formulæ, to every notion
of time and space, to everything that is established
such as customs, institutions, the church ; a feeling
at one's ease in a world in which no sign of reality
is any longer visible, a merely "inner" world, a
"true" world, an "eternal" world. . . . "The Kingdom of God is within you.". . .

30

The instinctive hatred of reality is the outcome of
an extreme susceptibility to pain and to irritation,
which can no longer endure to be "touched" at all,
because every sensation strikes too deep.

*The instinctive exclusion of all aversion, of all hos-
tility, of all boundaries and distances in feeling,* is the
outcome of an extreme susceptibility to pain and to
irritation, which regards all resistance, all compul-
sory resistance as insufferable *anguish* (—that is to

say, as harmful, as *deprecated* by the self-preservative
instinct), and which knows blessedness (happiness)
only when it is no longer obliged to offer resistance
to anybody, either evil or detrimental,—love as the
only ultimate possibility of life. . . .

These are the two *physiological realities* upon which
and out of which the doctrine of salvation has grown.
I call them a sublime further development of hedon-
ism, upon a thoroughly morbid soil. Epicureanism,
the pagan theory of salvation, even though it possessed a large proportion of Greek vitality and
nervous energy, remains the most closely related to
the above. Epicurus was a *typical* decadent: and
I was the first to recognise him as such.—The terror
of pain, even of infinitely slight pain—such a state
cannot possibly help culminating in a *religion* of
love. . . .

31

I have given my reply to the problem in advance.
The prerequisite thereto was the admission of the
fact that the type of the Saviour has reached us
only in a very distorted form. This distortion in
itself is extremely feasible : for many reasons a type
of that kind could not be pure, whole, and free from
additions. The environment in which this strange
figure moved, must have left its mark upon him, and
the history, the *destiny* of the first Christian communities must have done so to a still greater degree.
Thanks to that destiny, the type must have been
enriched retrospectively with features which can be
interpreted only as serving the purposes of war and
of propaganda. That strange and morbid world into
which the gospels lead us—a world which seems to

have been drawn from a Russian novel, where the
scum and dross of society, diseases of the nerves
and "childish" imbecility seem to have given each
other rendezvous—must in any case have *coarsened*
the type: the first disciples especially must have
translated an existence conceived entirely in symbols and abstractions into their own crudities, in
order at least to be able to understand something
about it,—for them the type existed only after it
had been cast in a more familiar mould. . . . The
prophet, the Messiah, the future judge, the teacher
of morals, the thaumaturgist, John the Baptist—all
these were but so many opportunities of misunderstanding the type. . . . Finally, let us not under-
rate the *proprium* of all great and especially sectarian
veneration : very often it effaces from the venerated
object, all the original and frequently painfully un-
familiar traits and idiosyncrasies—*it does not even see
them.* It is greatly to be deplored that no Dostoi-
ewsky lived in the neighbourhood of this most interesting decadent,—I mean someone who would
have known how to feel the poignant charm of such
a mixture of the sublime, the morbid, and the child-
like. Finally, the type, as an example of decadence,
may actually have been extraordinarily multifarious
and contradictory : this, as a possible alternative, is
not to be altogether ignored. Albeit, everything
seems to point away from it; for, precisely in this
case, tradition would necessarily have been particularly true and objective : whereas we have reasons
for assuming the reverse. Meanwhile a yawning
chasm of contradiction separates the mountain, lake,
and pastoral preacher, who strikes us as a Buddha

on a soil only very slightly Hindu, from that com-
bative fanatic, the mortal enemy of theologians and
priests, whom Renan's malice has glorified as "*le
grand maître en ironie.*" For my part, I do not
doubt but what the greater part of this venom (and
even of *esprit*) was inoculated into the type of the
Master only as the outcome of the agitated condition of Christian propaganda. For we have ample
reasons for knowing the unscrupulousness of all
sectarians when they wish to contrive their own
apology out of the person of their master. When
the first Christian community required a discerning,
wrangling, quarrelsome, malicious and hair-splitting
theologian, to oppose other theologians, it created
its "God" according to its needs; just as it did not
hesitate to put upon his lips those utterly unevangelical ideas of "his second coming," the "last judgment,"—ideas with which it could not then dispense,
—and every kind of expectation and promise which
happened to be current.

32

I can only repeat that I am opposed to the
importation of the fanatic into the type of the
Saviour: the word "*impérieux,*" which Renan uses,
in itself annuls the type. The "glad tidings" are
simply that there are no longer any contradictions,
that the Kingdom of Heaven is for the *children;*
the faith which raises its voice here is not a faith
that has been won by a struggle,—it is to hand, it
was there from the beginning, it is a sort of spiritual
return to childishness. The case of delayed and
undeveloped puberty in the organism, as the result

of degeneration is at least familiar to physiologists.
A faith of this sort does not show anger, it does not
blame, neither does it defend itself: it does not
bring "the sword,"—it has no inkling of how it will
one day establish feuds between man and man. It
does not demonstrate itself, either by miracles, or
by reward and promises, or yet "through the scriptures": it is in itself at every moment its own
miracle, its own reward, its own proof, its own
"Kingdom of God." This faith cannot be formulated—it lives, it guards against formulæ. The
accident of environment, of speech, of preparatory
culture, certainly determines a particular series of
conceptions: early Christianity deals only in Judæo-
Semitic conceptions (—the eating and drinking at
the last supper form part of these,—this idea which
like everything Jewish has been abused so mali-
ciously by the church). But one should guard
against seeing anything more than a language of
signs, semeiotics, an opportunity for parables in all
this. The very fact that no word is to be taken
literally, is the only condition on which this Anti-
realist is able to speak at all. Among Indians he
would have made use of the ideas of Sankhyam,
among Chinese, those of Lao-tze—and would not
have been aware of any difference. With a little
terminological laxity Jesus might be called a "free
spirit"—he cares not a jot for anything that is
established: the word *killeth*, everything fixed
killeth. The idea, *experience*, "life" as he alone
knows it, is, according to him, opposed to every
kind of word, formula, law, faith and dogma. He
speaks only of the innermost things: "life" or

"truth," or "light," is his expression for the innermost thing,—everything else, the whole of reality, the whole of nature, language even, has only the value of a sign, of a simile for him.—It is of paramount importance not to make any mistake at this point, however great may be the temptation thereto that lies in Christian — I mean to say, ecclesiastical prejudice. Any such essential symbolism stands beyond the pale of all religion, all notions of cult, all history, all natural science, all experience of the world, all knowledge, all politics, all psychology, all books and all Art—for his "wisdom" is precisely the complete ignorance * of the existence of such things. He has not even heard speak of *culture*, he does not require to oppose it,—he does not deny it. . . . The same holds good of the state, of the whole of civil and social order, of work and of war—he never had any reason to deny the world, he had not the vaguest notion of the ecclesiastical concept "the world." . . . Denying is precisely what was quite impossible to him.—Dialectic is also quite absent, as likewise the idea that any faith, any "truth" can be proved by argument (—his proofs are inner "lights," inward feelings of happiness and self-affirmation, a host of "proofs of power"—). Neither can such a doctrine contradict, it does not even realise the fact that there are or can be other doctrines, it is absolutely incapable of imagining a contrary judgment. . . . Wherever it encounters such things, from a feeling of profound sympathy it

* "*reine Thorheit*" in the German text, referring once again to Parsifal.—Tr.

bemoans such "blindness,"—for it sees the "light,"
—but it raises no objections.

33

The whole psychology of the "gospels" lacks
the concept of guilt and punishment, as also that
of reward. "Sin," any sort of aloofness between
God and man, is done away with,—*this is precisely
what constitutes the "glad tidings."* Eternal bliss
is not promised, it is not bound up with certain
conditions; it is the only reality—the rest consists
only of signs wherewith to speak about it. . . .

The results of such a state project themselves
into a new practice of life, the actual evangelical
practice. It is not a "faith" which distinguishes
the Christians: the Christian acts, he distinguishes
himself by means of a *different* mode of action.
He does not resist his enemy either by words or
in his heart. He draws no distinction between
foreigners and natives, between Jews and Gentiles
("the neighbour" really means the co-religionist,
the Jew). He is angry with no one, he despises no
one. He neither shows himself at the tribunals nor
does he acknowledge any of their claims ("Swear
not at all"). He never under any circumstances
divorces his wife, even when her infidelity has been
proved.—All this is at bottom one principle, it is all
the outcome of one instinct.—

The life of the Saviour was naught else than
this practice,—neither was his death. He no longer
required any formulæ, any rites for his relations
with God—not even prayer. He has done with all

the Jewish teaching of repentance and of atonement;
he alone knows the *mode* of life which makes one
feel "divine," "saved," "evangelical," and at all
times a "child of God." *Not* "repentance," *not*
"prayer and forgiveness" are the roads to God:
the *evangelical mode of life alone* leads to God, it *is*
"God."—That which the gospels abolished was the
Judaism of the concepts "sin," "forgiveness of
sin," "faith," "salvation through faith,"—the whole
doctrine of the Jewish church was denied by the
"glad tidings."

The profound instinct of how one must live in
order to feel "in Heaven," in order to feel "eternal,"
while in every other respect one feels by *no* means
"in Heaven": this alone is the psychological reality
of "Salvation."—A new life and *not* a new faith. . . .

34

If I understand anything at all about this great
symbolist, it is this that he regarded only *inner*
facts as facts, as "truths,"—that he understood the
rest, everything natural, temporal, material and
historical, only as signs, as opportunities for parables.
The concept "the Son of Man," is not a concrete
personality belonging to history, anything individual
and isolated, but an "eternal" fact, a psychological
symbol divorced from the concept of time. The
same is true, and in the highest degree, of the *God*
of this typical symbolist, of the "Kingdom of God,"
of the "Kingdom of Heaven," and of the "Sonship
of God." Nothing is more un-Christlike than the
ecclesiastical crudity of a personal God, of a King-

dom of God that is coming, of a "Kingdom of Heaven" beyond, of a "Son of God" as the second person of the Trinity. All this, if I may be forgiven the expression, is as fitting as a square peg in a round hole—and oh! what a hole!—the gospels: a *world-historic* cynicism in the scorn of symbols. . . . But what is meant by the signs "Father" and "Son," is of course obvious—not to everybody, I admit: with the word "Son," *entrance* into the feeling of the general transfiguration of all things (beatitude) is expressed, with the word "Father," *this feeling itself*, the feeling of eternity and of perfection.—I blush to have to remind you of what the Church has done with this symbolism: has it not set an Amphitryon story at the threshold of the Christian "faith"? And a dogma of immaculate conception into the bargain? . . . *But by so doing it defiled conception.— —*

The "Kingdom of Heaven" is a state of the heart —not something which exists "beyond this earth" or comes to you "after death." The whole idea of natural death is lacking in the gospels. Death is not a bridge, not a means of access: it is absent because it belongs to quite a different and merely apparent world the only use of which is to furnish signs, similes. The "hour of death" is not a Christian idea—the "hour," time in general, physical life and its crises do not exist for the messenger of "glad tidings." . . . The "Kingdom of God" is not something that is expected ; it has no yesterday nor any day after to-morrow, it is not going to come in a "thousand years"—it is an experience of a human heart ; it is everywhere, it is nowhere. . . .

35

This " messenger of glad tidings " died as he lived
and as he taught—*not* in order " to save mankind,"
but in order to show how one ought to live.   It was
a mode of life that he bequeathed to mankind : his
behaviour before his judges, his attitude towards his
executioners, his accusers, and all kinds of calumny
and scorn,—his demeanour on the *cross*.   He offers
no resistance; he does not defend his rights; he
takes no step to ward off the most extreme consequences, he does more,—he provokes them.   And
he prays, suffers and loves with those, in those, who
treat him ill. . . . *Not* to defend one's self, *not* to
show anger, not to hold anyone responsible. . . .
But to refrain from resisting even the evil one,—to
love him. . . .

36

—Only we spirits that have *become free*, possess
the necessary condition for understanding something
which nineteen centuries have misunderstood,—that
honesty which has become an instinct and a passion
in us, and which wages war upon the "holy lie" with
even more vigour than upon every other lie. . . .
Mankind was unspeakably far from our beneficent
and cautious neutrality, from that discipline of the
mind, which, alone, renders the solution of such
strange and subtle things possible : at all times, with
shameless egoism, all that people sought was their
own advantage in these matters, the Church was
built up out of contradiction to the gospel. . . .
Whoever might seek for signs pointing to the
guiding fingers of an ironical deity behind the great

comedy of existence, would find no small argument
in the *huge note of interrogation* that is called
Christianity. The fact that mankind is on its knees
before the reverse of that which formed the origin,
the meaning and the *rights* of the gospel; the fact
that, in the idea "Church," precisely that is pronounced holy which the "messenger of glad tidings"
regarded as *beneath* him, as *behind* him — one might
seek in vain for a more egregious example of *world-
historic* irony.— —

37

—Our age is proud of its historical sense : how
could it allow itself to be convinced of the nonsensi-
cal idea that at the beginning Christianity consisted
only of the *clumsy fable of the thaumaturgist and of
the Saviour*, and that all its spiritual and symbolic
side was only developed later? On the contrary :
the history of Christianity—from the death on the
cross onwards—is the history of a gradual and ever
coarser misunderstanding of an original symbolism.
With every extension of Christianity over ever
larger and ruder masses, who were ever less able to
grasp its first principles, the need of *vulgarising and
barbarising* it increased proportionately—it absorbed
the teachings and rites of all the *subterranean* cults
of the *imperium Romanum*, as well as the nonsense
of every kind of morbid reasoning. The fatal
feature of Christianity lies in the necessary fact that
its faith had to become as morbid, base and vulgar
as the needs to which it had to minister were morbid,
base and vulgar. *Morbid barbarism* at last braces
itself together for power in the form of the Church

—the Church, this deadly hostility to all honesty,
to all loftiness of the soul, to all discipline of the
mind, to all frank and kindly humanity.—*Christian*
and *noble* values : only we spirits *who have become
free* have re-established this contrast in values which
is the greatest that has ever existed on earth !—

38

—I cannot, at this point, stifle a sigh.   There are
days when I am visited by a feeling blacker than
the blackest melancholy—the *contempt of man.*   And
in order that I may leave you in no doubt as to
what I despise, *whom* I despise : I declare that it is
the man of to-day, the man with whom I am fatally
contemporaneous.   The man of to-day, I am as-
phyxiated by his foul breath. . . . Towards the
past, like all knights of knowledge, I am profoundly
tolerant,—that is to say, I exercise a sort of *generous*
self-control : with gloomy caution I pass through
whole millennia of this mad-house world, and
whether it be called "Christianity," "Christian
Faith," or "Christian Church," I take care not to
hold mankind responsible for its mental disorders.
But my feeling suddenly changes, and vents itself
the moment I enter the modern age, *our* age.   Our
age *knows*. . . . That which formerly was merely
morbid, is now positively indecent.   It is indecent
nowadays to be a Christian.   *And it is here that my
loathing begins.*   I look about me : not a word of
what was formerly known as "truth" has remained
standing ; we can no longer endure to hear a priest
even pronounce the word "truth."   Even he who

makes but the most modest claims upon truth, *must* know at present, that a theologian, a priest, or a pope, not only errs but actually *lies*, with every word that he utters,—and that he is no longer able to lie from "innocence," from "ignorance." Even the priest knows quite as well as everybody else does that there is no longer any "God," any "sinner" or any "Saviour," and that "free will," and "a moral order of the universe" are *lies*. Seriousness, the profound self-conquest of the spirit no longer allows anyone to be *ignorant* about this. . . . All the concepts of the Church have been revealed in their true colours—that is to say, as the most vicious frauds on earth, calculated to *depreciate* nature and all natural values. The priest himself has been recognised as what he is—that is to say, as the most dangerous kind of parasite, as the actual venomous spider of existence. . . . At present we know, our *conscience* knows, the real value of the gruesome inventions which the priests and the Church have made, *and what end they served.* By means of them that state of self-profanation on the part of man has been attained, the sight of which makes one heave. The concepts "Beyond," "Last Judgment," "Immortality of the Soul," the "soul" itself, are merely so many instruments of torture, so many systems of cruelty, on the strength of which the priest became and remained master. . . . Everybody knows this, *and nevertheless everything remains as it was.* Whither has the last shred of decency, of self-respect gone, if nowadays even our statesmen—a body of men who are otherwise so unembarrassed, and such thorough anti-Christians in deed—still declare themselves

Christians and still flock to communion?* . . .
Fancy a prince at the head of his legions, magnificent as the expression of the egoism and self-
exaltation of his people,—but *shameless* enough to
acknowledge himself a Christian ! . . . What then
does Christianity deny? What does it call "world"?
"The world" to Christianity means that a man is
a soldier, a judge, a patriot, that he defends himself,
that he values his honour, that he desires his own
advantage, that he is *proud*. . . . The conduct of
every moment, every instinct, every valuation that
leads to a deed, is at present anti-Christian : what
an *abortion of falsehood* modern man must be, in
order to be able *without a blush* still to call himself
a Christian !— —

39

—I will retrace my steps, and will tell you the
genuine history of Christianity.—The very word
"Christianity" is a misunderstanding,—truth to
tell, there never was more than one Christian,
and he *died* on the Cross. The "gospel" *died* on
the cross. That which thenceforward was called
"gospel" was the reverse of that "gospel" that
Christ had lived : it was "evil tidings," a *dysangel*.
It is false to the point of nonsense to see in "faith,"
in the faith in salvation through Christ, the dis-
tinguishing trait of the Christian : the only thing
that is Christian is the Christian mode of existence,
a life such as he led who died on the Cross. . . .
To this day a life of this kind is still possible ; for

* This applies apparently to Bismarck, the forger of the
Ems telegram and a sincere Christian.—Tr.

certain men, it is even necessary: genuine, primitive Christianity will be possible in all ages. . . . *Not* a faith, but a course of action, above all a course of inaction, non-interference, and a different life. . . . States of consciousness, any sort of faith, a holding of certain things for true, as every psychologist knows, are indeed of absolutely no consequence, and are only of fifth-rate importance compared with the value of the instincts: more exactly, the whole concept of intellectual causality is false. To reduce the fact of being a Christian, or of Christianity, to a holding of something for true, to a mere phenomenon of consciousness, is tantamount to denying Christianity. *In fact there have never been any Christians.* The "Christian," he who for two thousand years has been called a Christian, is merely a psychological misunderstanding of self. Looked at more closely, there ruled in him, *notwithstanding* all his faith, only instincts —and *what instincts !*—" Faith " in all ages, as for instance in the case of Luther, has always been merely a cloak, a pretext, a *screen*, behind which the instincts played their game,—a prudent form of *blindness* in regard to the dominion of *certain* instincts. . . . " Faith " I have already characterised as a piece of really Christian cleverness; for people have always spoken of " faith " and acted according to their instincts. . . . In the Christian's world of ideas there is nothing which even touches reality: but I have already recognised in the instinctive hatred of reality the actual motive force, the only driving power at the root of Christianity. What follows therefrom ? That here, even *in psychologicis*,

error is fundamental,—that is to say capable of
determining the spirit of things,—that is to say,
substance. Take one idea away from the whole,
and put one realistic fact in its stead,—and the
whole of Christianity tumbles into nonentity!—
Surveyed from above, this strangest of all facts,—
a religion not only dependent upon error, but in-
ventive and showing signs of genius only in those
errors which are dangerous and which poison life
and the human heart—remains a *spectacle for gods*,
for those gods who are at the same time philosophers and whom I met for instance in those
celebrated dialogues on the island of Naxos. At
the moment when they get rid of their *loathing*
(—*and we do as well!*), they will be thankful for
the spectacle the Christians have offered: the
wretched little planet called Earth perhaps deserves
on account of *this* curious case alone, a divine
glance, and divine interest. . . . Let us not therefore underestimate the Christians: the Christian,
false *to the point of innocence in falsity*, is far above
the apes,—in regard to the Christians a certain
well-known theory of Descent becomes a mere
good-natured compliment.

40

—The fate of the gospel was decided at the
moment of the death,—it hung on the "cross." . . .
It was only death, this unexpected and ignominious
death; it was only the cross which as a rule was
reserved simply for the *canaille*,—only this appalling
paradox which confronted the disciples with the
actual riddle: *Who was that? what was that?*—

The state produced by the excited and profoundly wounded feelings of these men, the suspicion that such a death might imply the *refutation* of their cause, and the terrible note of interrogation : "why precisely thus ? " will be understood only too well. In this case everything *must* be necessary, everything must have meaning, a reason, the highest reason. The love of a disciple admits of no such thing as accident. Only then did the chasm yawn : "who has killed him ? " "who was his natural enemy ? "—this question rent the firmament like a flash of lightning. Reply : *dominant* Judaism, its ruling class. Thenceforward the disciple felt himself in revolt *against* established order; he understood Jesus, after the fact, as one in *revolt against established order.* Heretofore this warlike, this nay-saying and nay-doing feature in Christ had been lacking ; nay more, he was its contradiction. The small primitive community had obviously understood *nothing* of the principal factor of all, which was the example of freedom and of superiority to every form of *resentment* which lay in this way of dying. And this shows how little they understood him altogether ! At bottom Jesus could not have desired anything else by his death than to give the strongest public *example* and *proof* of his doctrine. . . . But his disciples were very far from *forgiving* this death—though if they had done so it would have been in the highest sense evangelical on their part,—neither were they prepared, with a gentle and serene calmness of heart, to *offer* themselves for a similar death. . . . Precisely the most unevangelical feeling, *revenge*, became once more

ascendant.   It was impossible for the cause to end
with this death : " compensation " and " judgment "
were required (—and forsooth, what could be more
unevangelical than " compensation," " punishment,"
" judgment " !)   The popular expectation of a Messiah once more became prominent ; attention was
fixed upon one historical moment : the " Kingdom
of God " descends to sit in judgment upon his
enemies.   But this proves that everything was
misunderstood : the " Kingdom of God " regarded
as the last scene of the last act, as a promise !   But
the Gospel had clearly been the living, the fulfil-
ment, the *reality* of this " Kingdom of God."   It
was precisely a death such as Christ's that was this
" Kingdom of God."   It was only now that all the
contempt for the Pharisees and the theologians, and
all bitter feelings towards them, were introduced
into the character of the Master,—and by this means
he himself was converted into a Pharisee and a
theologian !   On the other hand, the savage veneration of these completely unhinged souls could no
longer endure that evangelical right of every man
to be the child of God, which Jesus had taught :
their revenge consisted in *elevating* Jesus in a
manner devoid of all reason, and in separating him
from themselves : just as, formerly, the Jews, with
the view of revenging themselves on their enemies,
separated themselves from their God, and placed
him high above them.   The Only God, and the Only
Son of God :—both were products of resentment.

41

—And from this time forward an absurd problem

rose into prominence: "how *could* God allow it to happen?" To this question the disordered minds of the small community found a reply which in its absurdity was literally terrifying: God gave his Son as a *sacrifice* for the forgiveness of sins. Alas! how prompt and sudden was the end of the gospel! Expiatory sacrifice for guilt, and indeed in its most repulsive and barbaric form,—the sacrifice of the *innocent* for the sins of the guilty! What appalling Paganism!—For Jesus himself had done away with the concept "guilt,"—he denied any gulf between God and man, he *lived* this unity between God and man, it was this that constituted *his* "glad tidings." ... And he did *not* teach it as a privilege!—Thenceforward there was gradually imported into the type of the Saviour the doctrine of the Last Judgment, and of the "second coming," the doctrine of sacrificial death, and the doctrine of *Resurrection*, by means of which the whole concept "blessedness," the entire and only reality of the gospel, is conjured away—in favour of a state *after* death! ... St Paul, with that rabbinic impudence which characterises all his doings, rationalised this conception, this prostitution of a conception, as follows: "if Christ did not rise from the dead, our faith is vain."—And, in a trice, the most contemptible of all unrealisable promises, the *impudent* doctrine of personal immortality, was woven out of the gospel. ... St Paul even preached this immortality as a reward.

42

You now realise what it was that came to an end with the death on the cross: a new and thoroughly

original effort towards a Buddhistic movement of
peace, towards real and *not* merely promised *happiness on earth*.   For, as I have already pointed out,
this remains the fundamental difference between the
two religions of *decadence:* Buddhism promises little
but fulfils more, Christianity promises everything
but fulfils nothing.—The "glad tidings" were followed closely by the absolutely *worst* tidings—those
of St Paul.   Paul is the incarnation of a type which
is the reverse of that of the Saviour ; he is the genius
in hatred, in the standpoint of hatred, and in the
relentless logic of hatred.   And alas what did this
dysangelist not sacrifice to his hatred !   Above all
the Saviour himself: he nailed him to *his* cross.
Christ's life, his example, his doctrine and death, the
sense and the right of the gospel—not a vestige of
all this was left, once this forger, prompted by his
hatred, had understood in it only that which could
serve his purpose.   *Not* reality : *not* historical truth!
. . . And once more, the sacerdotal instinct of
the Jew, perpetrated the same great crime against
history,—he simply cancelled the yesterday, and the
day before that, out of Christianity ; he *contrived of
his own accord a history of the birth of Christianity.*
He did more : he once more falsified the history of
Israel, so as to make it appear as a prologue to
his mission : all the prophets had referred to *his*
"Saviour." . . . Later on the Church even distorted
the history of mankind so as to convert it into
a prelude to Christianity. . . . The type of the
Saviour, his teaching, his life, his death, the meaning
of his death, even the sequel to his death—nothing
remained untouched, nothing was left which even

remotely resembled reality. St Paul simply trans-
ferred the centre of gravity of the whole of that
great life, to a place *behind* this life,—in the *lie* of
the "resuscitated" Christ. At bottom, he had no
possible use for the life of the Saviour,—he needed
the death on the cross, *and* something more. To
regard as honest a man like St Paul (a man whose
home was the very headquarters of Stoical enlighten-
ment) when he devises a proof of the continued
existence of the Saviour out of a hallucination ; or
even to believe him when he declares that he had
this hallucination, would amount to foolishness on
the part of a psychologist : St Paul desired the end,
consequently he also desired the means. . . . Even
what he himself did not believe, was believed in by
the idiots among whom he spread *his* doctrine.—
What he wanted was power ; with St Paul the priest
again aspired to power,—he could make use only of
concepts, doctrines, symbols with which masses may
be tyrannised over, and with which herds are formed.
What was the only part of Christianity which was
subsequently borrowed by Muhamed ? St Paul s
invention, his expedient for priestly tyranny and to
the formation of herds : the belief in immortality—
that is to say, the doctrine of the "Last Judgment." . . .

43

When the centre of gravity of life is laid, *not* in
life, but in a beyond—*in nonentity,*—life is utterly
robbed of its balance. The great lie of personal
immortality destroys all reason, all nature in the
instincts,—everything in the instincts that is beneficent, that promotes life and that is a guarantee

of the future, henceforward aroused suspicion.
The very meaning of life is now construed as the
effort to live in such a way that life no longer has
any point. . . . Why show any public spirit? Why
be grateful for one's origin and one's forebears?
Why collaborate with one's fellows, and be confident? Why be concerned about the general weal
or strive after it? . . . All these things are merely
so many "temptations," so many deviations from the
" straight path." " One thing only is necessary." . . .
That everybody, as an " immortal soul," should have
equal rank, that in the totality of beings, the " salvation " of each individual may lay claim to eternal
importance, that insignificant bigots and three-
quarter-lunatics may have the right to suppose that
the laws of nature may be persistently *broken* on
their account,—any such magnification of every
kind of selfishness to infinity, to *insolence*, cannot
be branded with sufficient contempt. And yet it
is to this miserable flattery of personal vanity that
Christianity owes its *triumph*,—by this means it
lured all the bungled and the botched, all revolt-
ing and revolted people, all abortions, the whole of
the refuse and offal of humanity, over to its side.
The "salvation of the soul"—in plain English:
"the world revolves around me." . . . The poison
of the doctrine " *equal* rights for all "—has been
dispensed with the greatest thoroughness by Christianity: Christianity, prompted by the most secret
recesses of bad instincts, has waged a deadly war
upon all feeling of reverence and distance between
man and man—that is to say, the *prerequisite* of
all elevation, of every growth in culture; out of

the resentment of the masses it wrought its *princi-pal weapons* against us, against everything noble, joyful, exalted on earth, against our happiness on earth. . . . To grant "immortality" to every St Peter and St Paul, was the greatest, the most vicious out-rage upon *noble* humanity that has ever been perpe-trated.—And do not let us underestimate the fatal influence which, springing from Christianity, has insinuated itself even into politics! Nowadays no one has the courage of special rights, of rights of dominion, of a feeling of self-respect and of respect for his equals,—of *pathos of distance*. Our politics are diseased with this lack of courage!—The aristo-cratic attitude of mind has been most thoroughly undermined by the lie of the equality of souls; and if the belief in the "privilege of the greatest number" creates and will continue *to create revolu-tions*,—it is Christianity, let there be no doubt about it, and Christian values, which convert every revolution into blood and crime! Christianity is the revolt of all things that crawl on their bellies against everything that is lofty: the gospel of the "lowly" *lowers*. . . .

44

—The Gospels are invaluable as a testimony of the corruption which was already persistent *within* the first Christian communities. That which St Paul, with the logician's cynicism of a Rabbi, carried to its logical conclusion, was nevertheless merely the process of decay which began with the death of the Saviour.—These gospels cannot be read too cautiously; difficulties lurk behind every word they

contain. I confess, and people will not take this
amiss, that they are precisely on that account a joy
of the first rank for a psychologist,—as the reverse
of all naïve perversity, as refinement *par excellence*,
as a masterpiece of art in psychological corruption.
The gospels stand alone. Altogether the Bible
allows of no comparison. The *first* thing to be
remembered if we do not wish to lose the scent here,
is, that we are among Jews. The dissembling of
holiness which, here, literally amounts to genius,
and which has never been even approximately
achieved elsewhere either by books or by men, this
fraud in word and pose which in this book is
elevated to an *Art*, is not the accident of any
individual gift, of any exceptional nature. These
qualities are a matter of *race*. With Christianity,
the art of telling holy lies, which constitutes the
whole of Judaism, reaches its final mastership, thanks
to many centuries of Jewish and most thoroughly
serious training and practice. The Christian, this
ultima ratio of falsehood, is the Jew over again—he
is even three times a Jew. . . . The fundamental
will only to make use of concepts, symbols and
poses, which are demonstrated by the practice of
the priests, the instinctive repudiation of every other
kind of practice, every other standpoint of valuation
and of utility — all this is not only tradition, it is
hereditary : only as an inheritance is it able to work
like nature. The whole of mankind, the best brains,
and even the best ages—(one man only excepted
who is perhaps only a monster)—have allowed themselves to be deceived. The gospels were read as
the *book of innocence* . . . this is no insignificant

sign of the virtuosity with which deception has been
practised here.—Of course, if we could only succeed
in seeing all these amazing bigots and pretended
saints, even for a moment, all would be at an end—
and it is precisely because *I* can read no single word
of theirs, without seeing their pretentious poses,
that I have made an end of them. . . . I cannot
endure a certain way they have of casting their eyes
heavenwards.—Fortunately for Christianity, books
are for the greatest number, merely *literature.* We
must not let ourselves be led away : "judge not!"
they say, but they dispatch all those to hell who
stand in their way. Inasmuch as they let God
do the judging, they themselves judge ; inasmuch
as they glorify God, they glorify themselves ; inasmuch as they *exact* those virtues of which they themselves happen to be capable — nay more, of which
they are in need in order to be able to remain on
top at all ;—they assume the grand airs of struggling
for virtue, of struggling for the dominion of virtue.
"We live, we die, we sacrifice ourselves for the
good " (—"the Truth," "the Light," "the Kingdom
of God"): as a matter of fact they do only what
they cannot help doing. Like sneaks they have to
play a humble part ; sit away in corners, and remain
obscurely in the shade, and they make all this appear
a *duty :* their humble life now appears as a duty,
and their humility is one proof the more of their
piety. . . . Oh, what a humble, chaste and compas-
sionate kind of falsity ! " Virtue itself shall bear us
testimony." . . . Only read the gospels as books
calculated to seduce by means of morality : morality
is appropriated by these petty people,—they know

what morality can do! The best way of leading mankind by the nose is with morality! The fact is that the most conscious *conceit* of people who believe themselves to be *chosen*, here simulates modesty: in this way they, the Christian community, the " good and the just " place themselves once and for all on a certain side, the side " of Truth "—and the rest of mankind, " the world " on the other. . . . This was the most fatal kind of megalomania that had ever yet existed on earth: insignificant little abortions of bigots and liars began to lay sole claim to the concepts " God," " Truth," " Light," " Spirit," " Love," " Wisdom," " Life," as if these things were, so to speak, synonyms of themselves, in order to fence themselves off from " the world " ; little ultra-Jews, ripe for every kind of madhouse, twisted values round in order to suit themselves, just as if the Christian, alone, were the meaning, the salt, the standard and even the " *ultimate tribunal*" of all the rest of mankind. . . . The whole fatality was rendered possible only because a kind of megalomania, akin to this one and allied to it in race,—the Jewish kind—was already to hand in the world : the very moment the gulf between Jews and Judæo-Christians was opened, the latter had no alternative left, but to adopt the same self-preservative measures as the Jewish instinct suggested, even *against* the Jews themselves, whereas the Jews, theretofore, had employed these same measures only against the Gentiles. The Christian is nothing more than an anarchical Jew.

45

—Let me give you a few examples of what these

paltry people have stuffed into their heads, what
they have laid *on the lips of their Master*: quite
a host of confessions from "beautiful souls."—

"And whosoever shall not receive you, nor hear
you, when ye depart thence, shake off the dust
under your feet for a testimony against them.
Verily I say unto you, It shall be more tolerable
for Sodom and Gomorrah in the day of judgment, than for that city." (Mark vi. 11.)—*How
evangelical!* . . .

"And whosoever shall offend one of these little
ones that believe in me, it is better for him that
a millstone were hanged about his neck, and he
were cast into the sea." (Mark ix. 42.)—How
evangelical! . . .

"And if thine eye offend thee, pluck it out: it is
better for thee to enter into the kingdom of God
with one eye, than having two eyes to be cast into
hell fire: where their worm dieth not, and the fire
is not quenched." (Mark ix. 47, 48.)—The eye is not
precisely what is meant in this passage. . . .

"Verily I say unto you, That there be some of
them that stand here, which shall not taste of death,
till they have seen the kingdom of God come with
power." (Mark ix. 1.)—Well *lied*, lion!* . . .

"Whosoever will come after me, let him deny
himself, and take up his cross, and follow me.
For . . ." (*A psychologist's comment.* Christian
morality is refuted by its "For's": its "reasons"
refute,—this is Christian.) (Mark viii. 34.)

---

* An adaptation of Shakespeare's "Well roared, lion"
(*Mid. N. D.*, Act 5, Sc. i.), the lion, as is well known, being
the symbol for St Mark in Christian literature and Art.—TR.

"Judge not, that ye be not judged. For with what judgment ye judge, ye shall be judged.' (Matthew vii. 1, 2.)—What a strange notion of justice on the part of a "just" judge! . . .

" For if ye love them which love you, what reward have ye? do not even the publicans the same? And if ye salute your brethren only, what do ye more *than others?* do not even the publicans so?" (Matthew v. 46, 47.) The principle of "Christian love": it insists upon being *well paid.* . . .

"But if ye forgive not men their trespasses neither will your Father forgive your trespasses." (Matthew vi. 15.)—Very compromising for the "Father" in question.

"But seek ye first the kingdom of God, and his righteousness; and all these things shall be added unto you." (Matthew vi. 33.)—"All these things" —that is to say, food, clothing, all the necessities of life. To use a moderate expression, this is an *error.* . . . Shortly before this God appears as a tailor, at least in certain cases. . . .

" Rejoice ye in that day, and leap for joy: for, behold, your reward *is* great in heaven: for in the like manner did their fathers unto the prophets." (Luke vi. 23.)—*Impudent* rabble! They dare to compare themselves with the prophets. . . .

"Know ye not that ye are the temple of God and *that* the Spirit of God dwelleth in you? If any man defile the temple of God, *him shall God destroy;* for the temple of God is holy, which *temple ye are.*" (St Paul, 1 Corinthians iii. 16, 17.) —One cannot have too much contempt for this sort of thing. . . .

"Do ye not know that the saints shall judge the world? and if the world shall be judged by you, are ye unworthy to judge the smallest matters?" (St Paul, 1 Corinthians vi. 2.)—Unfortunately this is not merely the speech of a lunatic. . . . This *appalling impostor* proceeds thus: "Know ye not that we shall judge angels? how much more things that pertain to this life?"

"Hath not God made foolish the wisdom of this world? For after that in the wisdom of God, the world by wisdom knew not God, it pleased God by the foolishness of preaching to save them that believe . . . not many wise men after the flesh, not many mighty, not many noble *are called:* But God hath chosen the foolish things of the world to confound the wise; and God hath chosen the weak things of the world to confound the things which are mighty; And base things of the world, and things which are despised, hath God chosen; *yea,* and things which are not, to bring to nought things that are: That no flesh should glory in his presence." (St Paul, 1 Corinthians i. 20 *et seq.*)—In order to *understand* this passage, which is of the highest importance as an example of the psychology of every Chandala morality, the reader should refer to my *Genealogy of Morals:* in this book, the contrast between a *noble* and a Chandala morality born of *resentment* and impotent revengefulness, is brought to light for the first time. St Paul was the greatest of all the apostles of revenge. . . .

46

What follows from this? That one does well to

put on one's gloves when reading the New Testament. The proximity of so much pitch almost defiles one. We should feel just as little inclined to hobnob with "the first Christians" as with Polish Jews: not that we need explain our objections. . . . They simply smell bad.—In vain have I sought for a single sympathetic feature in the New Testament; there is not a trace of freedom, kindliness, open-heartedness and honesty to be found in it. Humaneness has not even made a start in this book, while *cleanly* instincts are entirely absent from it. . . . Only evil instincts are to be found in the New Testament, it shows no sign of courage, these people lack even the courage of their evil instincts. All is cowardice, all is a closing of one's eyes and self-deception. Every book becomes clean, after one has just read the New Testament: for instance, immediately after laying down St Paul, I read with particular delight that most charming and most wanton of scoffers, Petronius, of whom someone might say what Domenico Boccaccio wrote to the Duke of Parma about Cæsar Borgia: "*è tutto festo*" —immortally healthy, immortally cheerful and well-constituted. . . . These petty bigots err in their calculations and in the most important thing of all. They certainly attack; but everything they assail is, by that very fact alone, *distinguished*. He whom a "primitive Christian" attacks, is *not* thereby sullied. . . . Conversely it is an honour to be opposed by "primitive Christians." One cannot read the New Testament without feeling a preference for everything in it which is the subject of abuse—not to speak of the "wisdom of this world,"

which an impudent windbag tries in vain to confound "by the foolishness of preaching." Even the
Pharisees and the Scribes derive advantage from
such opposition: they must certainly have been
worth something in order to have been hated in such
a disreputable way. Hypocrisy—as if this were a
reproach which the "first Christians" *were at liberty*
to make!—After all the Scribes and Pharisees were
the *privileged ones:* this was quite enough, the hatred
of the Chandala requires no other reasons. I very
much fear that the "first Christian"—as also the
"*last Christian*" *whom I may yet be able to meet,*—
is in his deepest instincts a rebel against everything
privileged; he lives and struggles unremittingly for
"equal rights"!... Regarded more closely, he
has no alternative.... If one's desire be person-
ally to represent "one of the chosen of God"—or
a "temple of God," or "a judge of angels,"—then
every *other* principle of selection, for instance that
based upon a standard of honesty, intellect, manli-
ness and pride, or upon beauty and freedom of heart,
becomes the "world,"—*evil in itself.* Moral: every
word on the lips of a "first Christian" is a lie, every
action he does is an instinctive falsehood,—all his
values, all his aims are pernicious; but the man he
hates, *the thing* he hates, *has value.*... The Christian, more particularly the Christian priest, is a
criterion of values— —Do I require to add that in the
whole of the New Testament only *one* figure appears
which we cannot help respecting? Pilate, the Roman
Governor. To take a Jewish quarrel *seriously* was
a thing he could not get himself to do. One Jew
more or less—what did it matter?... The noble

scorn of a Roman, in whose presence the word
"truth" had been shamelessly abused, has enriched
the New Testament with the only saying which *is
of value*,—and this saying is not only the criticism,
but actually the shattering of that Testament:
"What is truth!" . . .

47

—That which separates us from other people is
not the fact that we can discover no God, either in
history, or in nature, or behind nature,—but that we
regard what has been revered as "God," not as
"divine," but as wretched, absurd, pernicious; not
as an error, but as a *crime against life*. . . . We
deny God as God. . . . If the existence of this
Christian God were *proved* to us, we should feel even
less able to believe in him.—In a formula: *deus
qualem Paulus creavit, dei negatio*.—A religion such
as Christianity which never once comes in touch
with reality, and which collapses the very moment
reality asserts its rights even on one single point,
must naturally be a mortal enemy of the "wisdom
of this world"—that is to say, *science*. It will call
all those means good with which mental discipline,
lucidity and severity in intellectual matters, nobility
and freedom of the intellect may be poisoned, calum-
niated and *decried*. "Faith" as an imperative is
a *veto* against science,—*in praxi*, it means lies at
any price. St Paul *understood* that falsehood—that
"faith" was necessary; subsequently the Church
understood St Paul.—That "God" which St Paul
invented for himself, a God who "confounds" the
"wisdom of this world" (in a narrower sense, the

two great opponents of all superstition, philology and medicine), means, in very truth, simply St Paul's firm *resolve* to do so: to call his own will "God", *thora*, that is arch-Jewish. St Paul insists upon confounding the "wisdom of this world": his enemies are the *good old* philologists and doctors of the Alexandrine schools; it is on them that he wages war. As a matter of fact no one is either a philologist or a doctor, who is not also an *Antichrist*. As a philologist, for instance, a man sees *behind* the "holy books," as a doctor he sees *behind* the physiological rottenness of the typical Christian. The doctor says "incurable," the philologist says "forgery."

48

—Has anybody ever really understood the celebrated story which stands at the beginning of the Bible,—concerning God's deadly panic over *science?* ... Nobody has understood it. This essentially sacerdotal book naturally begins with the great inner difficulty of the priest: *he* knows only one great danger, *consequently* "God" has only one great danger.—

The old God, entirely "spirit," a high-priest through and through, and wholly perfect, is wandering in a leisurely fashion round his garden; but he is bored. Against boredom even the gods themselves struggle in vain.* What does he do? He invents man,—man is entertaining. ... But, behold,

---

* A parody on a line in Schiller's "*Jungfrau von Orleans*" (Act 3, Sc. vi.): "*Mit der Dummheit kämpfen Götter selbst vergebens*" (With stupidity even the gods themselves struggle in vain).—TR.

even man begins to be bored. God's compassion for the only form of misery which is peculiar to all paradises, exceeds all bounds: so forthwith he creates yet other animals. God's *first* mistake : man did not think animals entertaining,—he dominated them, he did not even wish to be an "animal." Consequently God created woman. And boredom did indeed cease from that moment,—but many other things ceased as well! Woman was God's *second* mistake.—"Woman in her innermost nature is a serpent, Heva"—every priest knows this : "all evil came into this world through woman,"—every priest knows this too. "*Consequently science* also comes from woman." . . . Only through woman did man learn to taste of the tree of knowledge.—What had happened? Panic had seized the old God. Man himself had been his *greatest* mistake, he had created a rival for himself, science makes you *equal to God*,—it is all up with priests and gods when man becomes scientific!—Moral: science is the most prohibited thing of all,—it alone, is forbidden. Science is the *first*, the germ of all sins, the original sin. *This alone is morality.*—"Thou shalt *not* know":— the rest follows as a matter of course. God's panic did not deprive him of his intelligence. How can one *guard* against science? For ages this was his principal problem. Reply : man must be kicked out of paradise! Happiness, leisure leads to thinking,—all thoughts are bad thoughts. . . . Man *must* not think.—And the "priest-per-se" proceeds to invent distress, death, the vital danger of pregnancy, every kind of misery, decrepitude, and affliction, and above all *disease*,—all these are but weapons

employed in the struggle with science! Trouble
prevents man from thinking. . . . And notwithstanding all these precautions! Oh, horror! the
work of science towers aloft, it storms heaven itself,
it rings the death-knell of the gods,—what's to be
done ?—The old God invents *war ;* he separates the
nations, and contrives to make men destroy each
other mutually (—the priests have always been in
need of war . . .). War, among other things, is a
great disturber of science!—Incredible! Knowledge, *the rejection of the sacerdotal yoke,* nevertheless
increases. — So the old God arrives at this final
decision : " Man has become scientific,—*there is no
help for it, he must be drowned !* " . . .

49

You have understood me. The beginning of the
Bible contains the whole psychology of the priest.—
The priest knows only one great danger, and that
is science,—the healthy concept of cause and effect.
But, on the whole, science flourishes only under happy
conditions,—a man must have time, he must also
have superfluous mental energy in order to " pursue
knowledge." . . . " *Consequently* man must be made
unhappy,"—this has been the argument of the priest
of all ages.—You have already divined what, in accordance with such a manner of arguing, must first
have come into the world :—" sin." . . . The notion
of guilt and punishment, the whole " moral order of
the universe," was invented against science,—against
the deliverance of man from the priest. . . . Man
must *not* cast his glance upon the outer world, he
must turn it inwards into himself; he must not as

a learner look cleverly and cautiously *into* things ;
he must not see at all : he must *suffer*. . . . And
he must suffer, so that he may be in need of the
priest every minute.—Away with doctors ! What
is needed is a Saviour !—The notion of guilt and
punishment, including the doctrine of "grace," of
"salvation" and of "forgiveness"—all *lies* through
and through without a shred of psychological reality
—were invented in order to destroy man's *sense of
causality :* they are an attack on the concept of cause
and effect !—And *not* an attack with the fist, with
the knife, with honesty in hate and love ! But one
actuated by the most cowardly, most crafty, and
most ignoble instincts ! A *priest's* attack ! A *parasite's* attack ! A vampyrism of pale subterranean
leeches !— . . . When the natural consequences of an
act are no longer "natural," but are thought to be
conjured up by phantom concepts of superstition, by
"God," by "spirits," and by "souls," as merely moral
consequences, in the form of rewards, punishments,
hints, and educational means,—then the whole basis
of knowledge is destroyed,—*then the greatest crime
against man has been perpetrated.*—Sin, I repeat, this
form of self-pollution *par excellence* on the part of
man, was invented in order to make science, culture
and every elevation and noble trait in man quite
impossible ; by means of the invention of sin the
priest is able to *rule.*

50

—I cannot here dispense with a psychology of
"faith" and of the "faithful," which will naturally
be to the advantage of the "faithful." If to-day there

are still many who do not know how very *indecent*
it is to be a "believer"—*or* to what extent such a
state is the sign of decadence, and of the broken will
to Life,—they will know it no later than to-morrow.
My voice can make even those hear who are hard
of hearing.—If perchance my ears have not deceived
me, it seems that among Christians there is such a
thing as a kind of criterion of truth, which is called
"the proof of power."   "Faith saveth ; *therefore* it is
true."—It might be objected here that it is precisely
salvation which is not proved but only *promised :*
salvation is bound up with the condition " faith,"—
one *shall* be saved, *because* one has faith. . . . But
how prove *that* that which the priest promises
to the faithful really will take place, to wit : the
"Beyond" which defies all demonstration ?—The
assumed "proof of power" is at bottom once again
only a belief in the fact that the effect which faith
promises will not fail to take place.   In a formula :
"I believe that faith saveth ;—*consequently* it is true."
—But with this we are at the end of our tether.   This
"consequently" would be the *absurdum* itself as a
criterion of truth.—Let us be indulgent enough to
assume, however, that salvation is proved by faith
(—*not* only desired, and *not* merely promised by the
somewhat suspicious lips of a priest): could salvation
—or, in technical terminology, *happiness*—ever be a
proof of truth ?   So little is it so that, when pleasur-
able sensations make their influence felt in replying
to the question "what is true," they furnish almost
the contradiction of truth, or at any rate they
make it in the highest degree suspicious.   The proof
through "happiness," is a proof of happiness—and

nothing else ; why in the world should we take it for granted that *true* judgments cause more pleasure than false ones, and that in accordance with a pre-established harmony, they necessarily bring pleasant feelings in their wake ?—The experience of all strict and profound minds teaches the *reverse.* Every inch of truth has been conquered only after a struggle, almost everything to which our heart, our love and our trust in life cleaves, has had to be sacrificed for it. Greatness of soul is necessary for this : the service of truth is the hardest of all services.—What then is meant by honesty in things intellectual? It means that a man is severe towards his own heart, that he scorns " beautiful feelings," and that he makes a matter of conscience out of every Yea and Nay !— — —Faith saveth : *consequently* it lies. . . .

51

The fact that faith may in certain circumstances save, the fact that salvation as the result of an *idée fixe* does not constitute a true idea, the fact that faith moves *no* mountains, but may very readily raise them where previously they did not exist— all these things are made sufficiently clear by a mere casual stroll through a *lunatic asylum.* Of course *no* priest would find this sufficient : for he instinctively denies that illness is illness or that lunatic asylums are lunatic asylums. Christianity is in *need* of illness, just as Ancient Greece was in need of a superabundance of health. The actual ulterior motive of the whole of the Church's system of salvation is to *make people ill.* And is not the Church itself the Catholic madhouse as an ultimate ideal?—The earth as a whole converted into a madhouse?—The kind of religious man which the Church aims at producing is a typical *decadent*. The moment of time at which a religious crisis attains the ascendancy over a people, is always characterised by nerve-epidemics; the "inner world" of the religious man is ridiculously like the "inner world" of over-irritable and exhausted people; the "highest" states which Christianity holds up to mankind as the value of values, are epileptic in character,—the Church has pronounced only madmen *or* great swindlers *in majorem dei honorem* holy. Once I ventured to characterise the whole of the Christian training of penance and salvation (which nowadays is best studied in England) as a *folie circulaire* methodically generated upon a soil which, of course, is already prepared for it,—that is to say, which is thoroughly morbid. Not every one who likes can be a Christian: no man is "converted" to Christianity,—he must be sick enough for it. . . . We others who possess enough courage both for health and for contempt, how rightly *we* may despise a religion which taught men to misunderstand the body! which would not rid itself of the superstitions of the soul! which made a virtue of taking inadequate nourishment! which in health combats a sort of enemy, devil, temptation! which persuaded itself that it was possible to bear a perfect soul about in a cadaverous body, and which, to this end, had to make up for itself a new concept of "perfection," a pale, sickly, idiotically gushing ideal,—so-called "holiness,"— holiness, which in itself is simply a symptom of

an impoverished, enervated and incurably deterio-
rated body! . . . The movement of Christianity,
as a European movement, was from first to last, a
general accumulation of the ruck and scum of all
sorts and kinds (—and these, by means of Christianity, aspire to power). It does *not* express the
downfall of a race, it is rather a conglomerate
assembly of all the decadent elements from everywhere which seek each other and crowd together.
It was not, as some believe, the corruption of
antiquity, of *noble* antiquity, which made Christianity possible: the learned idiocy which nowadays
tries to support such a notion cannot be too severely
contradicted. At the time when the morbid and
corrupted Chandala classes became Christianised in
the whole of the *imperium,* the very *contrary type,*
nobility, was extant in its finest and maturest
forms. The greatest number became master; the
democracy of Christian instincts triumphed. . . .
Christianity was not "national," it was not determined by race,—it appealed to all the disinherited
forms of life, it had its allies everywhere. Christianity is built upon the rancour of the sick; its
instinct is directed *against* the sound, against
health. Everything well-constituted, proud, high-
spirited, and beautiful is offensive to its ears and
eyes. Again I remind you of St Paul's priceless
words: "And God hath chosen the *weak* things
of the world, the *foolish* things of the world; and
base things of the world, and things which are
despised": this was the formula, *in hoc signo* decadence triumphed.—*God on the Cross*—does no one
yet understand the terrible ulterior motive of this

symbol?—Everything that suffers, everything that
hangs on the cross, is *divine*. . . . All of us hang
on the cross, consequently we are *divine*. . . . We
alone are divine. . . . Christianity was a victory;
a *nobler* type of character perished through it,—
Christianity has been humanity's greatest misfortune hitherto.— —

52

Christianity also stands opposed to everything
happily constituted in the *mind*,—it can make use
only of morbid reason as Christian reason; it takes
the side of everything idiotic, it utters a curse upon
"intellect," upon the *superbia* of the healthy intellect.
Since illness belongs to the essence of Christianity,
the typically Christian state, "faith," *must* also be
a form of illness, and all straight, honest and scientific roads to knowledge must be repudiated by the
Church as forbidden. . . . Doubt in itself is already
a sin. . . . The total lack of psychological cleanliness in the priest, which reveals itself in his look, is
a *result* of decadence. Hysterical women, as also
children with scrofulous constitutions, should be
observed as a proof of how invariably instinctive
falsity, the love of lying for the sake of lying, and
the inability either to look or to walk straight, are the
expression of decadence. "Faith" simply means the
refusal to know what is true. The pious person, the
priest of both sexes, is false because he is ill:
his instinct *demands* that truth should not assert its
right anywhere. "That which makes ill is good:
that which proceeds from abundance, from superabundance and from power, is evil": that is the
view of the faithful. The *constraint to lie*—that is

the sign by which I recognise every predetermined
theologian.—Another characteristic of the theologian is his lack of *capacity* for *philology*. What
I mean here by the word philology is, in a general
sense to be understood as the art of reading well, of
being able to take account of facts *without* falsify-
ing them by interpretation, without losing either
caution, patience or subtlety owing to one's desire
to understand. Philology as *ephexis** in interpretation, whether one be dealing with books, news-
paper reports, human destinies or meteorological
records,—not to speak of the "salvation of the
soul." . . . The manner in which a theologian,
whether in Berlin or in Rome, interprets a verse
from the "Scriptures," or an experience, or the
triumph of his nation's army for instance, under the
superior guiding light of David's Psalms, is always
so exceedingly *daring*, that it is enough to make a
philologist's hair stand on end. And what is he to
do, when pietists and other cows from Swabia
explain their miserable every-day lives in their
smoky hovels by means of the "Finger of God," a
miracle of "grace," of "Providence," of experiences
of "salvation"! The most modest effort of the
intellect, not to speak of decent feeling, ought at
least to lead these interpreters to convince themselves of the absolute childishness and unworthiness
of any such abuse of the dexterity of God's fingers.
However small an amount of loving piety we might

* ἔφεξις = Lat. Retentio, Inhibitio (Stephanus, Thesaurus
Græcæ Linguæ) ; therefore : reserve, caution. The Greek
Sceptics were also called Ephectics owing to their caution in
judging and in concluding from facts.—TR.

possess, a god who cured us in time of a cold in the
nose, or who arranged for us to enter a carriage
just at the moment when a cloud burst over our
heads, would be such an absurd God, that he would
have to be abolished, even if he existed.*   God as a
domestic servant, as a postman, as a general provider,
—in short, merely a word for the most foolish kind of
accidents. . . . " Divine Providence," as it is believed
in to-day by almost every third man in " cultured
Germany," would be an argument against God, in
fact it would be the strongest argument against God
that could be imagined.   And in any case it is an
argument against the Germans.

53

—The notion that martyrs prove anything at all
in favour of a thing, is so exceedingly doubtful, that
I would fain deny that there has ever yet existed a
martyr who had anything to do with truth.   In the
very manner in which a martyr flings his little parcel
of truth at the head of the world, such a low degree
of intellectual honesty and such obtuseness in regard
to the question " truth " makes itself felt, that one
never requires to refute a martyr.   Truth is not a
thing which one might have and another be without:

* The following passage from Multatuli will throw light on
this passage :—

" Father :—' Behold, my son, how wisely Providence has
arranged everything !   This bird lays its eggs in its nest and
the young will be hatched just about the time when there
will be worms and flies with which to feed them.   Then they
will sing a song of praise in honour of the Creator who over-
whelms his creatures with blessings.'—

" Son :—' Will the worms join in the song, Dad ? ' ".—Tr.

only peasants or peasant-apostles, after the style of
Luther, can think like this about truth. You may
be quite sure, that the greater a man's degree of
conscientiousness may be in matters intellectual,
the more modest he will show himself on this point.
To *know* about five things, and with a subtle wave
of the hand to refuse to know *others*. . . . " Truth "
as it is understood by every prophet, every sectarian,
every free thinker, every socialist and every church-
man, is an absolute proof of the fact that these people
haven't even begun that discipline of the mind and
that process of self-mastery, which is necessary for
the discovery of any small, even exceedingly small
truth.—Incidentally, the deaths of martyrs have been
a great misfortune in the history of the world : they
led people astray. . . . The conclusion which all
idiots, women and common people come to, that
there must be something in a cause for which someone lays down his life (or which, as in the case of
primitive Christianity, provokes an epidemic of sacri-
fices),—this conclusion put a tremendous check upon
all investigation, upon the spirit of investigation and
of caution. Martyrs have *harmed* the cause of truth.
. . . Even to this day it only requires the crude fact
of persecution, in order to create an honourable
name for any obscure sect who does not matter in
the least. What? is a cause actually changed in
any way by the fact that some one has laid down his
life for it ? An error which becomes honourable, is
simply an error that possesses one seductive charm
the more : do you suppose, dear theologians, that
we shall give you the chance of acting the martyrs
for your lies?—A thing is refuted by being laid

respectfully on ice, and theologians are refuted in the same way. This was precisely the world-historic foolishness of all persecutors ; they lent the thing they combated a semblance of honour by conferring the fascination of martyrdom upon it. . . . Women still lie prostrate before an error to-day, because they have been told that some one died on the cross for it. *Is the cross then an argument ?*—But concerning all these things, one person alone has said what mankind has been in need of for thousands of years,—*Zarathustra.*

" Letters of blood did they write on the way they went, and their folly taught that truth is proved by blood.

" But blood is the very worst testimony of truth ; blood poisoneth even the purest teaching, and turneth it into delusion and into blood feuds.

" And when a man goeth through fire for his teaching—what does that prove ? Verily, it is more when out of one's own burning springeth one's own teaching."*

54

Do not allow yourselves to be deceived : great minds are sceptical. Zarathustra is a sceptic. Strength and the *freedom* which proceeds from the power and excessive power of the mind, *manifests* itself through scepticism. Men of conviction are of no account whatever in regard to any principles of value or of non-value. Convictions are prisons. They never see far enough, they do not look down from a sufficient height : but in order to have any

* " Thus Spake Zarathustra." The Priests.—Tr.

say in questions of value and non-value, a man must
see five hundred convictions *beneath* him,—*behind*
him. . . . A spirit who desires great things, and
who also desires the means thereto, is necessarily
a sceptic. Freedom from every kind of conviction
belongs to strength, to the *ability* to open one's eyes
freely. . . . The great passion of a sceptic, the basis
and power of his being, which is more enlightened
and more despotic than he is himself, enlists all his
intellect into its service; it makes him unscrupulous;
it even gives him the courage to employ unholy
means; in certain circumstances it even allows
him convictions. Conviction as a *means :* much is
achieved merely by means of a conviction. Great
passion makes use of and consumes convictions, it
does not submit to them—it knows that it is a
sovereign power. Conversely ; the need of faith, of
anything either absolutely affirmative or negative,
Carlylism (if I may be allowed this expression), is
the need of *weakness*. The man of beliefs, the " believer " of every sort and condition, is necessarily a
dependent man ;—he is one who cannot regard *himself* as an aim, who cannot postulate aims from the
promptings of his own heart. The " believer " does
not belong to himself, he can be only a means, he
must be *used up*, he is in need of someone who uses
him up. His instinct accords the highest honour to
a morality of self-abnegation : everything in him,
his prudence, his experience, his vanity, persuade
him to adopt this morality. Every sort of belief is
in itself an expression of self-denial, of self-estrange-
ment. . . . If one considers how necessary a regulat-
ing code of conduct is to the majority of people, a

code of conduct which constrains them and fixes
them from outside; and how control, or in a higher
sense, *slavery*, is the only and ultimate condition
under which the weak-willed man, and especially
woman, flourish; one also understands conviction,
"faith." The man of conviction finds in the latter
his *backbone.* To be *blind* to many things, to be
impartial about nothing, to belong always to a particular side, to hold a strict and necessary point of
view in all matters of values—these are the only
conditions under which such a man can survive at
all. But all this is the reverse of, the *antagonist*
of, the truthful man,—of truth. . . . The believer is
not at liberty to have a conscience for the question
"true" and "untrue": to be upright on *this* point
would mean his immediate downfall. The patho-
logical limitations of his standpoint convert the convinced man into the fanatic—Savonarola, Luther
Rousseau, Robespierre, Saint-Simon,—these are the
reverse type of the strong spirit that has become *free.*
But the grandiose poses of these *morbid* spirits, of
these epileptics of ideas, exercise an influence over
the masses,—fanatics are picturesque, mankind prefers to look at poses than to listen to reason.

55

One step further in the psychology of conviction
of "faith." It is already some time since I first
thought of considering whether convictions were not
perhaps more dangerous enemies of truth than lies
("Human All-too-Human," Part I, Aphs. 54 and
483). Now I would fain put the decisive question:

is there any difference at all between a lie and a conviction?—All the world believes that there is, but what in Heaven's name does not all the world believe! Every conviction has its history, its preliminary stages, its period of groping and of mistakes: it becomes a conviction only after it has *not* been one for a long time, only after it has *scarcely* been one for a long time. What? might not falsehood be the embryonic form of conviction?—At times all that is required is a change of personality: very often what was a lie in the father becomes a conviction in the son.—I call a lie, to refuse to see something that one sees, to refuse to see it exactly *as* one sees it: whether a lie is perpetrated before witnesses or not is beside the point.—The most common sort of lie is the one uttered to one's self; to lie to others is relatively exceptional. Now this refusal to see what one sees, this refusal to see a thing exactly as one sees it, is almost the first condition for all those who belong to a *party* in any sense whatsoever: the man who belongs to a party perforce becomes a liar. German historians, for instance, are convinced that Rome stood for despotism, whereas the Teutons introduced the spirit of freedom into the world: what difference is there between this conviction and a lie? After this is it to be wondered at, that all parties, including German historians, instinctively adopt the grandiloquent phraseology of morality,—that morality almost owes its *survival* to the fact that the man who belongs to a party, no matter what it may be, is in need of morality every moment?— " This is our conviction: we confess it to the whole

world, we live and die for it,—let us respect everything that has a conviction!"—I have actually
heard antisemites speak in this way.   On the
contrary, my dear sirs!   An antisemite does not
become the least bit more respectable because he
lies on principle. . . . Priests, who in such matters
are more subtle, and who perfectly understand the
objection to which the idea of a conviction lies
open—that is to say of a falsehood which is perpetrated on principle *because* it serves a purpose,
borrowed from the Jews the prudent measure of
setting the concept " God," " Will of God," " Revelation of God," at this place.   Kant, too, with his
categorical imperative, was on the same road : this
was his *practical* reason.—There are some questions
in which it is *not* given to man to decide between
true and false ; all the principal questions, all the
principal problems of value, stand beyond human
reason. . . . To comprehend the limits of reason—
this alone is genuine philosophy.   For what purpose
did God give man revelation?   Would God have
done anything superfluous?   Man cannot of his
own accord know what is good and what is evil,
that is why God taught man his will. . . . Moral :
the priest does *not* lie, such questions as "truth " or
"falseness" have nothing to do with the things
concerning which the priest speaks ; such things
do not allow of lying.   For, in order to lie, it
would be necessary to know *what* is true in this
respect.   But that is precisely what man cannot
know : hence the priest is only the mouthpiece of
God.—This sort of sacerdotal syllogism is by no
means exclusively Judaic or Christian ; the right

to lie and the *prudent measure* of "revelation" belongs to the priestly type, whether of decadent periods or of Pagan times (—Pagans are all those who say yea to life, and to whom "God" is the word for the great yea to all things). The "law," the "will of God," the "holy book," and inspiration.—All these things are merely words for the conditions under which the priest attains to power, and with which he maintains his power,— these concepts are to be found at the base of all sacerdotal organisations, of all priestly or philosophical and ecclesiastical governments. The " holy lie," which is common to Confucius, to the law-book of Manu, to Muhamed, and to the Christian church, is not even absent in Plato. "Truth is here"; this phrase means, wherever it is uttered: *the priest lies.* . . .

56

After all, the question is, to what *end* are falsehoods perpetrated? The fact that, in Christianity, "holy" ends are entirely absent, constitutes *my* objection to the means it employs. Its ends are only *bad* ends: the poisoning, the calumniation and the denial of life, the contempt of the body, the degradation and self-pollution of man by virtue of the concept sin,—consequently its means are bad as well.—My feelings are quite the reverse when I read the law-book of *Manu,* an incomparably superior and more intellectual work, which it would be a sin against the *spirit* even to *mention* in the same breath with the Bible. You will guess immediately why: it has a genuine philosophy behind it, *in* it, not merely an evil-smelling Jewish distillation of Rabbinism and superstition,—it gives something to chew even to the most fastidious psychologist. And, *not* to forget the most important point of all, it is fundamentally different from every kind of Bible: by means of it the *noble classes*, the philosophers and the warriors guard and guide the masses; it is replete with noble values, it is filled with a feeling of perfection, with a saying of yea to life, and a triumphant sense of well-being in regard to itself and to life,—the sun shines upon the whole book.— All those things which Christianity smothers with its bottomless vulgarity: procreation, woman, marriage, are here treated with earnestness, with reverence, with love and confidence. How can one possibly place in the hands of children and women, a book that contains those vile words: "to avoid fornication, let every man have his own wife, and let every woman have her own husband . . . it is better to marry than to burn."*   And is it decent to be a Christian so long as the very origin of man is Christianised,—that is to say, befouled, by the idea of the *immaculata conceptio?* . . . I know of no book in which so many delicate and kindly things are said to woman, as in the Law-Book of Manu; these old grey-beards and saints have a manner of being gallant to women which, perhaps, cannot be surpassed. "The mouth of a woman," says Manu on one occasion, "the breast of a maiden, the prayer of a child, and the smoke of the sacrifice, are always pure." Elsewhere he says: "there is nothing purer than the light of the sun, the shadow cast by a cow, air, water, fire and the breath of a maiden." And finally—perhaps this is also a holy lie:—"all the

* I Corinthians vii. 2, 9.—TR.

openings of the body above the navel are pure, all
those below the navel are impure. Only in a maiden is
the whole body pure."

57

The unholiness of Christian means is caught *in
flagranti*, if only the end aspired to by Christianity
be compared with that of the Law-Book of Manu ;
if only these two utterly opposed aims be put under
a strong light. The critic of Christianity simply cannot avoid making Christianity *contemptible.*—A Law-
Book like that of Manu comes into being like every
good law-book : it epitomises the experience, the
precautionary measures, and the experimental morality of long ages, it settles things definitely, it no
longer creates. The prerequisite for a codification
of this kind, is the recognition of the fact that the
means which procure authority for a *truth* to which
it has cost both time and great pains to attain, are
fundamentally different from those with which that
same truth would be proved. A law-book never
relates the utility, the reasons, the preliminary casuistry, of a law : for it would be precisely in this way
that it would forfeit its imperative tone, the " thou
shalt," the first condition of its being obeyed. The
problem lies exactly in this.—At a certain stage in
the development of a people, the most far-seeing
class within it (that is to say, the class that sees
farthest backwards and forwards), declares the experience of how its fellow-creatures ought to live—
i.e., can live—to be finally settled. Its object is, to
reap as rich and as complete a harvest as possible,
in return for the ages of experiment and *terrible* experience it has traversed. Consequently, that which

has to be avoided, above all, is any further experi-
mentation, the continuation of the state when values
are still fluid, the testing, choosing, and criticising
of values *in infinitum*. Against all this a double
wall is built up : in the first place, *Revelation*, which
is the assumption that the rationale of every law is
not human in its origin, that it was not sought and
found after ages of error, but that it is divine in its
origin, completely and utterly without a history, a
gift, a miracle, a mere communication. . . . And
secondly, *tradition*, which is the assumption that the
law has obtained since the most primeval times, that
it is impious and a crime against one's ancestors to
attempt to doubt it. The authority of law is established on the principles : God *gave* it, the ancestors
lived it.—The superior reason of such a procedure
lies in the intention to draw consciousness off step
by step from that mode of life which has been recognised as correct (*i.e.*, *proved* after enormous and
carefully examined experience), so that perfect auto-
matism of the instincts may be attained,—this being
the only possible basis of all mastery of every kind
of perfection in the Art of Life. To draw up a law-
book like Manu's, is tantamount to granting a people
mastership for the future, perfection for the future,—
the right to aspire to the highest Art of Life. *To
that end it must be made unconscious:* this is the
object of every holy lie.—*The order of castes*, the
highest, the dominating law, is only the sanction
of a *natural order*, of a natural legislation of the
first rank, over which no arbitrary innovation, no
"modern idea" has any power. Every healthy
society falls into three distinct types, which recipro-

cally condition one another and which gravitate
differently in the physiological sense; and each of
these has its own hygiene, its own sphere of work,
its own special feeling of perfection, and its own
mastership. It is Nature, not Manu, that separates
from the rest, those individuals preponderating in
intellectual power, those excelling in muscular
strength and temperament, and the third class which
is distinguished neither in one way nor the other,
the mediocre,—the latter as the greatest number,
the former as the *élite*. The superior caste—I call
them the *fewest*,—has, as the perfect caste, the privileges of the fewest : it devolves upon them to represent happiness, beauty and goodness on earth. Only
the most intellectual men have the right to beauty,
to the beautiful : only in them is goodness not weakness. *Pulchrum est paucorum hominum :* goodness
is a privilege. On the other hand there is nothing
which they should be more strictly forbidden than
repulsive manners or a pessimistic look, a look that
makes everything *seem ugly*,—or even indignation
at the general aspect of things. Indignation is
the privilege of the Chandala, and so is pessimism.
" *The world is perfect*"—that is what the instinct of
the most intellectual says, the yea-saying instinct;
"imperfection, every kind of *inferiority* to us, distance, the pathos of distance, even the Chandala
belongs to this perfection. " The most intellectual
men, as the *strongest* find their happiness where
others meet with their ruin: in the labyrinth, in
hardness towards themselves and others, in en-
deavour; their delight is self-mastery : with them
asceticism becomes a second nature, a need, an in-

stinct. They regard a difficult task as their privilege; to play with burdens which crush their fellows is to them a *recreation*. . . . Knowledge, a form of asceticism.—They are the most honourable kind of men: but that does not prevent them from being the most cheerful and most gracious. They rule, not because they will, but because they *are;* they are not at liberty to take a second place.—The second in rank are the guardians of the law, the custodians of order and of security, the noble warriors, the king, above all, as the highest formula of the warrior, the judge, and keeper of the law. The second in rank are the executive of the most intellectual, the nearest to them in duty, relieving them of all that is *coarse* in the work of ruling,—their retinue, their right hand, their best disciples. In all this, I repeat, there is nothing arbitrary, nothing "artificial," that which is *otherwise* is artificial,—by that which is otherwise, nature is put to shame. . . . The order of castes, and the order of rank merely formulates the supreme law of life itself; the differentiation of the three types is necessary for the maintenance of society, and for enabling higher and highest types to be reared,—the *inequality* of rights is the only condition of there being rights at all.—A right is a privilege. And in his way, each has his privilege. Let us not underestimate the privileges of the *mediocre*. Life always gets harder towards the summit,—the cold increases, responsibility increases. A high civilisation is a pyramid: it can stand only upon a broad base, its first prerequisite is a strongly and soundly consolidated mediocrity. Handicraft, commerce, agriculture, science, the greater part of

art,—in a word, the whole range of professional and
business callings, is compatible only with mediocre
ability and ambition ; such pursuits would be out
of place among exceptions, the instinct pertaining
thereto would oppose not only aristocracy but anarchy as well. The fact that one is publicly useful,
a wheel, a function, presupposes a certain natural
destiny: it is not *society*, but the only kind of *happiness*
of which the great majority are capable, that makes
them intelligent machines. For the mediocre it is a
joy to be mediocre ; in them mastery in one thing,
a speciality, is a natural instinct. It would be absolutely unworthy of a profound thinker to see any
objection in mediocrity *per se*. For in itself it is the
first essential condition under which exceptions are
possible ; a high culture is determined by it. When
the exceptional man treats the mediocre with more
tender care than he does himself or his equals, this
is not mere courtesy of heart on his part—but
simply his *duty*. . . . Whom do I hate most among
the rabble of the present day ? The socialistic
rabble, the Chandala apostles, who undermine the
working man's instinct, his happiness and his feeling
of contentedness with his insignificant existence,—
who make him envious, and who teach him revenge.
. . . The wrong never lies in unequal rights ; it lies
in the claim to equal rights. What is *bad* ? But I
have already replied to this : Everything that proceeds from weakness, envy and *revenge*.—The anarchist and the Christian are offspring of the same
womb. . . .

58

In point of fact, it matters greatly to what end

one lies : whether one preserves or *destroys* by means
of falsehood.   It is quite justifiable to bracket the
Christian and the *Anarchist* together : their object,
their instinct, is concerned only with destruction.
The proof of this proposition can be read quite
plainly from history : history spells it with appalling distinctness.   Whereas we have just seen a
religious legislation, whose object was to render the
highest possible means of making life *flourish*,
and of making a grand organisation of society,
eternal,—Christianity found its mission in putting
an end to such an organisation, *precisely because
life flourishes through it*.   In the one case, the net
profit to the credit of reason, acquired through long
ages of experiment and of insecurity, is applied use-
fully to the most remote ends, and the harvest,
which is as large, as rich and as complete as possible, is reaped and garnered : in the other case, on
the contrary, the harvest is *blighted* in a single night.
That which stood there, *ære perennius*, the *imperium Romanum*, the most magnificent form of
organisation, under difficult conditions, that has
ever been achieved, and compared with which everything that preceded, and everything which followed
it, is mere patchwork, gimcrackery, and dilettantism,
—those holy anarchists made it their " piety," to
destroy " the world "—that is to say, the *imperium
Romanum*, until no two stones were left standing
one on the other,—until even the Teutons and other
clodhoppers were able to become master of it.   The
Christian and the anarchist are both decadents ;
they are both incapable of acting in any other way
than disintegratingly, poisonously and witheringly,

like *blood-suckers ;* they are both actuated by an
instinct of *mortal hatred* of everything that stands
erect, that is great, that is lasting, and that is a
guarantee of the future. . . . Christianity was the
vampire of the *imperium Romanum,*—in a night
it shattered the stupendous achievement of the
Romans, which was to acquire the territory for a
vast civilisation which could *bide its time.*—Does no
one understand this yet? The *imperium Romanum*
that we know, and which the history of the Roman
province teaches us to know ever more thoroughly,
this most admirable work of art on a grand scale,
was the beginning, its construction was calculated
to prove its worth by millenniums,—unto this day
nothing has ever again been built in this fashion,
nor have men even dreamt since of building on this
scale *sub specie æterni !* — This organisation was
sufficiently firm to withstand bad emperors : the
accident of personalities must have nothing to do
with such matters — the *first* principle of all great
architecture. But it was not sufficiently firm to
resist the *corruptest* form of corruption, to resist the
Christians. . . . These stealthy canker-worms, which
under the shadow of night, mist and duplicity,
insinuated themselves into the company of every
individual, and proceeded to drain him of all seriousness for *real* things, of all his instinct for *realities ;*
this cowardly, effeminate and sugary gang have step
by step alienated all "souls" from this colossal
edifice,—those valuable, virile and noble natures
who felt that the cause of Rome was their own
personal cause, their own personal seriousness, their
own personal *pride.* The stealth of the bigot, the

secrecy of the conventicle, concepts as black as hell such as the sacrifice of the innocent, the *unio mystica* in the drinking of blood, above all the slowly kindled fire of revenge, of Chandala revenge —such things became master of Rome, the same kind of religion on the pre-existent form of which Epicurus had waged war. One has only to read Lucretius in order to understand what Epicurus combated, *not* Paganism, but " Christianity," that is to say the corruption of souls through the concept of guilt, through the concept of punishment and immortality. He combated the *subterranean* cults, the whole of latent Christianity—to deny immor- tality was at that time a genuine *deliverance*.—And Epicurus had triumphed, every respectable thinker in the Roman Empire was an Epicurean : *then St Paul appeared* . . . St Paul, the Chandala hatred against Rome, against " the world," the Jew, the eternal Jew *par excellence*, become flesh and genius. . . . What he divined was, how, by the help of the small sectarian Christian movement, independent of Judaism, a universal conflagration could be kindled ; how, with the symbol of the " God on the Cross," everything submerged, everything secretly insurrec- tionary, the whole offspring of anarchical intrigues could be gathered together to constitute an enor- mous power. " For salvation is of the Jews."— Christianity is the formula for the supersession, *and* epitomising of all kinds of subterranean cults, that of Osiris, of the Great Mother, of Mithras for example : St Paul's genius consisted in his discovery of this. In this matter his instinct was so certain, that, regardless of doing violence to truth, he laid the

ideas by means of which those Chandala religions
fascinated, upon the very lips of the " Saviour " he
had invented, and not only upon his lips,—that he
made out of him something which even a Mithras
priest could understand. . . . This was his moment
of Damascus : he saw that he had *need* of the belief
in immortality in order to depreciate " the world,"
that the notion of " hell " would become master of
Rome, that with a " Beyond " *this life* can be killed.
. . . Nihilist and Christian,—they rhyme in German,
and they do not only rhyme.

59

The whole labour of the ancient world *in vain :*
I am at a loss for a word which could express my
feelings at something so atrocious.—And in view
of the fact that its labour was only preparatory,
that with adamantine self-consciousness it laid the
substructure, alone, to a work which was to last
millenniums, the whole *significance* of the ancient
world was certainly in vain ! . . . What was the use
of the Greeks ? what was the use of the Romans ?
—All the prerequisites of a learned culture, all the
scientific methods already existed, the great and
peerless art of reading well had already been
established—that indispensable condition to tradition, to culture and to scientific unity ; natural
science hand in hand with mathematics and
mechanics was on the best possible road,—the
sense for facts, the last and most valuable of all
senses, had its schools, and its tradition was already
centuries old ! Is this understood ? Everything
essential had been discovered to make it possible

for work to be begun :—methods, and this cannot
be said too often, are the essential thing, also the
most difficult thing, while they moreover have to
wage the longest war against custom and indo-
lence. That which to-day we have successfully
reconquered for ourselves, by dint of unspeakable
self-discipline—for in some way or other all of us
still have the bad instincts, the Christian instincts,
in our body,—the impartial eye for reality, the
cautious hand, patience and seriousness in the
smallest details, complete *uprightness* in knowledge,—all this was already there; it had been
there over two thousand years before! And in
addition to this there was also that excellent and
subtle tact and taste! *Not* in the form of brain
drilling! *Not* in the form of "German" culture
with the manners of a boor! But incarnate, mani-
festing itself in men's bearing and in their instinct,
—in short constituting reality. . . . *All this in
vain!* In one night it became merely a memory!
—The Greeks! The Romans! Instinctive nobility,
instinctive taste, methodic research, the genius of
organisation and administration, faith, the *will* to
the future of mankind, the great *yea* to all things
materialised in the *imperium Romanum*, become
visible to all the senses, grand style no longer
manifested in mere art, but in reality, in truth, in
life.—And buried in a night, not by a natural
catastrophe! Not stamped to death by Teutons
and other heavy-footed vandals! But destroyed
by crafty, stealthy, invisible anæmic vampires!
Not conquered,—but only drained of blood! . . .
The concealed lust of revenge, miserable envy

become *master!* Everything wretched, inwardly
ailing, and full of ignoble feelings, the whole
Ghetto-world of souls, was in a trice *uppermost!*
—One only needs to read any one of the Christian
agitators—St Augustine, for instance,—in order to
realise, in order to *smell*, what filthy fellows came
to the top in this movement. You would deceive
yourselves utterly if you supposed that the leaders
of the Christian agitation showed any lack of understanding:—Ah! they were shrewd, shrewd to the
point of holiness were these dear old Fathers of
the Church! What they lack is something quite
different. Nature neglected them,—it forgot to
give them a modest dowry of decent, of respectable
and of *cleanly* instincts. . . . Between ourselves,
they are not even men. If Islam despises Christianity, it is justified a thousand times over; for
Islam presupposes men.

60

Christianity destroyed the harvest we might
have reaped from the culture of antiquity, later it
also destroyed our harvest of the culture of Islam.
The wonderful Moorish world of Spanish culture,
which in its essence is more closely related to *us*,
and which appeals more to our sense and taste
than Rome and Greece, was *trampled to death* (—I
do not say by what kind of feet), why?—because it
owed its origin to noble, to manly instincts, because
it said yea to life, even that life so full of the rare
and refined luxuries of the Moors! . . . Later on
the Crusaders waged war upon something before
which it would have been more seemly in them to

grovel in the dust,—a culture, beside which even
our Nineteenth Century would seem very poor and
very "senile."—Of course they wanted booty: the
Orient was rich. . . . For goodness' sake let us
forget our prejudices! Crusades—superior piracy,
that is all! German nobility—that is to say, a
Viking nobility at bottom, was in its element in
such wars: the Church was only too well aware of
how German nobility is to be won. . . . German
nobility was always the "Swiss Guard" of the
Church, always at the service of all the bad instincts
of the Church; but it was *well paid for it all.* . . .
Fancy the Church having waged its deadly war
upon everything noble on earth, precisely with the
help of German swords, German blood and courage!
A host of painful *questions* might be raised on this
point. German nobility scarcely takes a place in
the history o higher culture: the reason of this
is obvious Christianity, alcohol—the two *great*
means of corruption. As a matter of fact, choice
ought to be just as much out of the question between
Islam and Christianity, as between an Arab and a
Jew. The decision is already self-evident; nobody
is at liberty to exercise a choice in this matter. A
man is either of the Chandala or he is *not.* . . .
"War with Rome to the knife! Peace and friendship with Islam": this is what that great free
spirit, that genius among German emperors,—
Frederick the Second, not only felt but also *did.*
What? Must a German in the first place be a
genius, a free-spirit, in order to have *decent* feelings?
I cannot understand how a German was ever able
to have *Christian* feelings.

61

Here it is necessary to revive a memory which will be a hundred times more painful to Germans. The Germans have destroyed the last great harvest of culture which was to be garnered for Europe,— it destroyed the *Renaissance*. Does anybody at last understand, *will* anybody understand what the Renaissance was? *The transvaluation of Christian values*, the attempt undertaken with all means, all instincts and all genius to make the *opposite* values, the *noble* values triumph. . . . Hitherto there has been only *this* great war : there has never yet been a more decisive question than the Renaissance,—*my* question is the question of the Renaissance :—there has never been a more fundamental, a more direct and a more severe *attack*, delivered with a whole front upon the centre of the foe. To attack at the decisive quarter, at the very seat of Christianity, and there to place *noble* values on the throne,—that is to say, to *introduce* them into the instincts, into the most fundamental needs and desires of those sitting there. . . . I see before me a possibility perfectly magic in its charm and glorious colouring —it seems to me to scintillate with all the quivering grandeur of refined beauty, that there is an art at work within it which is so divine, so infernally divine, that one might seek through millenniums in vain for another such possibility ; I see a spectacle so rich in meaning and so wonderfully paradoxical to boot, that it would be enough to make all the gods of Olympus rock with immortal laughter,— *Cæsar Borgia as Pope*. . . . Do you understand me?

. . . Very well then, this would have been the triumph which *I* alone am longing for to-day :— this would have *swept* Christianity *away !*—What happened ? A German monk, Luther, came to Rome. This monk, with all the vindictive instincts of an abortive priest in his body, foamed with rage over the Renaissance in Rome. . . . Instead of, with the profoundest gratitude, understanding the vast miracle that had taken place, the overcoming of Christianity at its *headquarters,*—the fire of his hate knew only how to draw fresh fuel from this spectacle. A religious man thinks only of himself.—Luther saw the corruption of the Papacy when the very reverse stared him in the face : the old corruption, the *peccatum originale,* Christianity *no* longer sat upon the Papal chair ! But Life ! The triumph of Life ! The great yea to all lofty, beautiful and daring things ! . . . And Luther reinstated the Church ; he attacked it. The Renaissance thus became an event without meaning, a great *in vain !* —Ah these Germans, what have they not cost us already ! In vain—this has always been the achievement of the Germans.—The Reformation, Leibniz, Kant and so-called German philosophy, the Wars of Liberation, the Empire—in each case are in vain for something which had already existed, for something which *cannot be recovered.* . . . I confess it, these Germans are my enemies : I despise every sort of uncleanliness in concepts and valuations in them, every kind of cowardice in the face of every honest yea or nay. For almost one thousand years, now, they have tangled and confused everything they have laid their hands on ; they have on their

conscience all the half-measures, all the three-eighth
measures of which Europe is sick ; they also have
the most unclean, the most incurable, and the most
irrefutable kind of Christianity—Protestantism—on
their conscience. . . . If we shall never be able to
get rid of Christianity, the *Germans* will be to blame.

62

—With this I will now conclude and pronounce
my judgment. I *condemn* Christianity and confront
it with the most terrible accusation that an accuser
has ever had in his mouth. To my mind it is the
greatest of all conceivable corruptions, it has had
the will to the last imaginable corruption. The
Christian Church allowed. nothing to escape from
its corruption ; it converted every value into its
opposite, every truth into a lie, and every honest
impulse into an ignominy of the soul. Let anyone
dare to speak to me of its humanitarian blessings !
To *abolish* any sort of distress was opposed to its
profoundest interests ; its very existence depended
on states of distress ; it created states of distress in
order to make itself immortal. . . . The cancer germ
of sin, for instance : the Church was the first to en-
rich mankind with this misery !—The " equality of
souls before God," this falsehood, this *pretext* for the
rancunes of all the base-minded, this anarchist bomb
of a concept, which has ultimately become the revolution, the modern idea, the principle of decay of
the whole of social order,—this is *Christian* dyna-
mite. . . . The " humanitarian " blessings of Christianity ! To breed a self-contradiction, an art of
self-profanation, a will to lie at any price, an aversion,

a contempt of all good and honest instincts out of *humanitas !* Is this what you call the blessings of Christianity ?—Parasitism as the only method of the Church ; sucking all the blood, all the love, all the hope of life out of mankind with anæmic and sacred ideals. A " Beyond " as the will to deny all reality ; the cross as the trade-mark of the most subterranean form of conspiracy that has ever existed,—against health, beauty, well-constitutedness, bravery, intellect, kindliness of soul, *against Life itself.* . . .

This eternal accusation against Christianity I would fain write on all walls, wherever there are walls,—I have letters with which I can make even the blind see. . . . I call Christianity the one great curse, the one enormous and innermost perversion, the one great instinct of revenge, for which no means are too venomous, too underhand, too underground and too *petty*,—I call it the one immortal blemish of mankind. . . .

And *time* is reckoned from the *dies nefastus* upon which this fatality came into being—from the first day of Christianity !—*why not rather from its last day ?—From to-day ?*—Transvaluation of all Values ! . . .

GREAT MINDS PAPERBACK SERIES

ART

❏ Leonardo da Vinci—
   A Treatise on Painting

ECONOMICS

❏ Charlotte Perkins Gilman—
   Women and Economics:
   A Study of the Economic Relation
   between Women and Men
❏ John Maynard Keynes—
   The End of Laissez-Faire and
   The Economic Consequences
   of the Peace
❏ John Maynard Keynes—
   The General Theory of
   Employment, Interest, and Money
❏ John Maynard Keynes—
   A Tract on Monetary Reform
❏ Thomas R. Malthus—An Essay on
   the Principle of Population
❏ Alfred Marshall—
   Money, Credit, and Commerce
❏ Alfred Marshall—
   Principles of Economics
❏ Karl Marx—
   Theories of Surplus Value
❏ John Stuart Mill—Principles of
   Political Economy
❏ David Ricardo—Principles of
   Political Economy and Taxation
❏ Adam Smith—Wealth of Nations
❏ Thorstein Veblen—
   The Theory of the Leisure Class

HISTORY

❏ J. B. Bury—Freedom of Thought
❏ Edward Gibbon—On Christianity
❏ Alexander Hamilton, John Jay,
   and James Madison—
   The Federalist
❏ Herodotus—The History
❏ Charles Mackay—
   Extraordinary Popular Delusions
   and the Madness of Crowds
❏ Thomas Paine—The Crisis
❏ Thucydides—History of the
   Peloponnesian War

LAW

❏ John Austin—The Province of
   Jurisprudence Determined

LITERATURE

❏ Jonathan Swift—A Modest
   Proposal and Other Satires
❏ H. G. Wells—
   The Conquest of Time

POLITICS

❏ Walter Lippmann—
   A Preface to Politics

PSYCHOLOGY

❏ Sigmund Freud—Totem and Taboo

RELIGION/FREETHOUGHT

❏ Desiderius Erasmus—
   The Praise of Folly
❏ Thomas Henry Huxley—
   Agnosticism and Christianity and
   Other Essays
❏ Ernest Renan—The Life of Jesus
❏ Upton Sinclair—
   The Profits of Religion
❏ Elizabeth Cady Stanton—
   The Woman's Bible
❏ Voltaire—A Treatise on Toleration
   and Other Essays
❏ Andrew D. White—A History of
   the Warfare of Science with
   Theology in Christendom

SCIENCE

❏ Jacob Bronowski—
   The Identity of Man
❏ Nicolaus Copernicus—On the
   Revolutions of Heavenly Spheres
❏ Francis Crick—
   Of Molecules and Men
❏ Marie Curie—
   Radioactive Substances
❏ Charles Darwin—
   The Autobiography
   of Charles Darwin

- ❑ Charles Darwin—
    The Descent of Man
- ❑ Charles Darwin—
    The Origin of Species
- ❑ Charles Darwin—
    The Voyage of the Beagle
- ❑ René Descartes—*Treatise of Man*
- ❑ Albert Einstein—*Relativity*
- ❑ Michael Faraday—
    The Forces of Matter
- ❑ Galileo Galilei—*Diálogues
    Concerning Two New Sciences*
- ❑ Francis Galton—*Finger Prints*
- ❑ Francis Galton—
    Hereditary Genius
- ❑ Ernst Haeckel—
    The Riddle of the Universe
- ❑ William Harvey—*On the Motion
    of the Heart and Blood in Animals*
- ❑ Fred Hoyle—*Of Men and Galaxies*
- ❑ Julian Huxley—
    Evolutionary Humanism
- ❑ Thomas H. Huxley—
    Evolution and Ethics and
    Science and Morals
- ❑ Edward Jenner—
    Vaccination against Smallpox

- ❑ Johannes Kepler—*Epitome of
    Copernican Astronomy*
    and *Harmonies of the World*
- ❑ James Clerk Maxwell—
    Matter and Motion
- ❑ Isaac Newton—*Opticks, Or
    Treatise of the Reflections,
    Inflections, and Colours of Light*
- ❑ Isaac Newton—*The Principia*
- ❑ Louis Pasteur and Joseph Lister—
    *Germ Theory and Its Applications
    to Medicine* and *On the Antiseptic
    Principle of the Practice of Surgery*
- ❑ Moritz Schlick—*Space and Time
    in Contemporary Physics*
- ❑ William Thomson (Lord Kelvin)
    and Peter Guthrie Tait—
    *The Elements of Natural
    Philosophy*
- ❑ Alfred Russel Wallace—
    Island Life

SOCIOLOGY

- ❑ Emile Durkheim—*Ethics and the
    Sociology of Morals*

GREAT BOOKS IN PHILOSOPHY PAPERBACK SERIES

ESTHETICS

- ❑ Aristotle—*The Poetics*
- ❑ Aristotle—*Treatise on Rhetoric*

ETHICS

- ❑ Aristotle—
    The Nicomachean Ethics
- ❑ Marcus Aurelius—*Meditations*
- ❑ Jeremy Bentham—*The Principles
    of Morals and Legislation*
- ❑ John Dewey—
    Human Nature and Conduct
- ❑ John Dewey—*The Moral Writings
    of John Dewey, Revised Edition*
- ❑ Epictetus—*Enchiridion*
- ❑ David Hume—*An Enquiry
    Concerning the Principles
    of Morals*
- ❑ Immanuel Kant—
    *Fundamental Principles of the
    Metaphysic of Morals*

- ❑ John Stuart Mill—*Utilitarianism*
- ❑ George Edward Moore—
    Principia Ethica
- ❑ Friedrich Nietzsche—
    Beyond Good and Evil
- ❑ Plato—*Protagoras, Philebus,* and
    Gorgias
- ❑ Bertrand Russell—*Bertrand Russell
    On Ethics, Sex, and Marriage*
- ❑ Arthur Schopenhauer—
    The Wisdom of Life and *Counsels
    and Maxims*
- ❑ Adam Smith—
    The Theory of Moral Sentiments
- ❑ Benedict de Spinoza—
    *Ethics including
    The Improvement of the
    Understanding*

LOGIC

- ❑ George Boole—
    The Laws of Thought

METAPHYSICS/EPISTEMOLOGY

- ❏ Aristotle—*De Anima*
- ❏ Aristotle—*The Metaphysics*
- ❏ Francis Bacon—*Essays*
- ❏ George Berkeley—*Three Dialogues Between Hylas and Philonous*
- ❏ W. K. Clifford—*The Ethics of Belief and Other Essays*
- ❏ René Descartes—*Discourse on Method* and *The Meditations*
- ❏ John Dewey—*How We Think*
- ❏ John Dewey—*The Influence of Darwin on Philosophy and Other Essays*
- ❏ Epicurus—*The Essential Epicurus: Letters, Principal Doctrines, Vatican Sayings, and Fragments*
- ❏ Sidney Hook—*The Quest for Being*
- ❏ David Hume—*An Enquiry Concerning Human Understanding*
- ❏ David Hume—*A Treatise on Human Nature*
- ❏ William James—*The Meaning of Truth*
- ❏ William James—*Pragmatism*
- ❏ Immanuel Kant—*The Critique of Judgment*
- ❏ Immanuel Kant—*Critique of Practical Reason*
- ❏ Immanuel Kant—*Critique of Pure Reason*
- ❏ Gottfried Wilhelm Leibniz—*Discourse on Metaphysics and the Monadology*
- ❏ John Locke—*An Essay Concerning Human Understanding*
- ❏ George Herbert Mead—*The Philosophy of the Present*
- ❏ Michel de Montaigne—*Essays*
- ❏ Charles S. Peirce—*The Essential Writings*
- ❏ Plato—*The Euthyphro, Apology, Crito,* and *Phaedo*
- ❏ Plato—*Lysis, Phaedrus,* and *Symposium*
- ❏ Bertrand Russell—*The Problems of Philosophy*
- ❏ George Santayana—*The Life of Reason*
- ❏ Arthur Schopenhauer—*On the Principle of Sufficient Reason*
- ❏ Sextus Empiricus—*Outlines of Pyrrhonism*
- ❏ Alfred North Whitehead—*The Concept of Nature*
- ❏ Ludwig Wittgenstein—*Wittgenstein's Lectures: Cambridge, 1932–1935*

PHILOSOPHY OF RELIGION

- ❏ Jeremy Bentham—*The Influence of Natural Religion on the Temporal Happiness of Mankind*
- ❏ Marcus Tullius Cicero—*The Nature of the Gods* and *On Divination*
- ❏ Ludwig Feuerbach—*The Essence of Christianity*
- ❏ Ludwig Feuerbach—*The Essence of Religion*
- ❏ Paul Henri Thiry, Baron d'Holbach—*Good Sense*
- ❏ David Hume—*Dialogues Concerning Natural Religion*
- ❏ William James—*The Varieties of Religious Experience*
- ❏ John Locke—*A Letter Concerning Toleration*
- ❏ Lucretius—*On the Nature of Things*
- ❏ John Stuart Mill—*Three Essays on Religion*
- ❏ Friedrich Nietzsche—*The Antichrist*
- ❏ Thomas Paine—*The Age of Reason*
- ❏ Bertrand Russell—*Bertrand Russell On God and Religion*

SOCIAL AND POLITICAL PHILOSOPHY

- ❏ Aristotle—*The Politics*
- ❏ Mikhail Bakunin—*The Basic Bakunin: Writings, 1869–1871*
- ❏ Jeremy Bentham—*The Rationale of Punishment*
- ❏ Edmund Burke—*Reflections on the Revolution in France*